Pennsylvania Dutch

The Plain and the Fancy

Pennsylvania Dutch

the plain and the fancy

by Scott Francis Brenner

The Stackpole Company
Harrisburg, Pennsylvania

Printed and bound
in the United States of America
by The Telegraph Press,
Established 1831
Harrisburg, Pennsylvania

Contents

The Preface

Pennsylvania Dutch—The Plain and The Fancy—you can see them at the Stock Yards in Lancaster, Pennsylvania, any day of the week except Sunday. You can see them in the Farmer's Market at Reading, York, Harrisburg, Allentown and a hundred other places any Friday or Saturday. You will see them at country sales, in the fields, at family reunions or at Church—almost any place in Dutch Pennsylvania. And, believe me, they are worth going to see. Visit them whenever you can. Meantime won't you lift the latch and let them visit you? That is what will happen as you turn the pages of *Pennsylvania Dutch— The Plain and The Fancy*.

Pennsylvania was founded as a place where all people might live happily together. In a sense, everyone belongs here, and soon everyone feels at home in Pennsylvania. The first to come were the Swedes, the English Quakers, and the Germans. Soon the Germans outnumbered and outdistanced their fellow immigrants. The descendants of these German pioneers are now called the Pennsylvania Dutch. The story can be summed up by saying these Dutch were here "firstest with the mostest," and it is they who have breathed the breath of life into Dutch Pennsylvania.

I have had the good fortune to live in Dutch Pennsylvania— to get the feel of it, to imbibe its spirit, to know it, and to love it. It is a love I would share with others. So here is the story, a true story with authentic places and real people. Only on occasion have I felt obliged to embroider a homespun tale with a touch of editorial lace, and only in those incidents where someone might be embarrassed have I changed the real names. As they say in the old country stores, "It's all wool and a yard wide."

While the story is mine, I freely confess that I could not have fathered it without the help of many friends. For one thing, my pen is not half as Dutch as my heart, and I know beyond doubt that the dialectical expressions are not always "chust so." In order that they may be tolerably near the mark I have had the manuscript read by the late Vincent Godshall, a direct descendant of the first American Mennonite Bishop; the Reverend Charles E. Schaeffer, D.D., beloved "Parre" of the old

Reformed Church; Dr. Fred Kring of Grove City College and his wife Hilda Adam Kring of Slippery Rock State Teachers College, and by Mr. and Mrs. Irwin Mayberry of Schwenksville, members of my first Dutch parish.

Moreover, it would not have been possible for me to put the story together without the stimulus of The Pennsylvania Dutch Folklore Center and without years of friendly contacts within the Pennsylvania German Society—which once honored me as a Director and as its Secretary—and the Pennsylvania German Folklore Society. The publications of these two societies have been most helpful. I make bold to single out three: *Pennsylvania German Illuminated Manuscripts* by Henry S. Borneman, *Consider the Lilies How They Grow* by John Joseph Stoudt, and *The Old Order Amish of Lancaster County* by Calvin George Bachman.

The art work has been done by Mr. John Johns, a staff artist for the *Pittsburgh Press*. He has long been interested in Pennsylvania Dutch folk art, as well he might, since his people originated in Syria and have been nurtured in the Orthodox Church. It was in the Near East that the Biblical faith was first clothed in art forms. In time these symbols pollinated the Mediterranean area and moved up into the heartland of Europe by way of the Danube, and finally into Pennsylvania by way of Penn's "Holy Experiment."

I am most in debt, however, to George Swetnam of the *Pittsburgh Press*, who has "swet" it out with me, prodding and guiding each step of the way. And there is Helen, my beloved wife, who has done so much of the hard "pick and shovel" work, and who, as might be expected, has always had the last word to say.

Now that you have come to the last of the preface turn the page and make yourself at home amongst your Pennsylvania Dutch visitors.

SCOTT FRANCIS BRENNER

1—A Hand Upon
Your Shoulder

THERE'S an oil painting down Bucks County way, a kind of Pennsylvania Dutch "Angelus." It's potato picking time and already the bittersweet is showing on the old stake-and-rider fence. In the background is a stately Church with a white colonial spire: Lutheran or Reformed, there can be little question about that. Everywhere there are potatoes, some in bags, others in piles; and several women are bending low as they doggedly pursue their menial task. The foreground is monopolized by a team of sleek horses hitched to a plow. Behind the plow is a young man with his shoulders stooped, his head bent low, as though all the cares of the world were heaped upon his back. Standing by his side is an older farmer who has long wintered the chill and disappointments of life and yet somehow manages to radiate confidence and good cheer. His hand is upon that young man's shoulder in a friendly sort of way.

Again and again in the Dutch country I've seen that hand upon the shoulder. I've seen it as the men tarried after Church; as they awaited the day's threshing; as they frolicked before the hoedown; as they laughed and joked at the picnic; as they waited in the hospital lobby; as they bowed at the open grave. The Pennsylvania Dutch are a friendly people. While it is true they are inhibited by a certain reserve that in the eyes of the stranger sometimes makes them appear aloof, in reality they have a consuming desire for the friendly way of life.

The Pennsylvania story begins not with William Penn, as we have so often been led to believe, but with his pious mother, Margaret Jasper, daughter of a wealthy merchant family in Rotterdam. Margaret Jasper was rich in this world's goods, but her chief treasure was in the world of the spirit. Her people had come under the religious impact of Menno Simons, who held to a simple faith of love toward God and man, a faith that made religion a matter of the heart and the way of life one of purity and peace. In order to share in this down-to-earth Christianity one must have nothing to do with pride or prestige or power or strife. It demands a pure heart and a meek soul. This emphasis of Menno Simons was seconded by such spiritual giants as Casper Schwenkfeld of Silesia, and Jacob Boehme, the inspired shoemaker of Goerlitz.

The structure of the Christian religion has tended to develop into two different patterns. The one lays great store upon outward form and organization while it emphasizes the universal truths—such is the broad, catholic way. There is another pattern, more inward and more narrow: the way of the sects. Each sect, or little group of believers, tends to glory in its own peculiar truth and to exalt its own distinctive virtues. They rejoice when "two or three are gathered together."

These sectarians usually become separatists. They believe in their own narrow way so strongly that they will have little to do with others who walk in a different way. Their tolerance is limited; their zeal is great. The New England Puritans are one example. Some of the Dutch "Saints" of Pennsylvania are another.

The sympathies of Margaret Jasper Penn were with those who walk in the narrow way. She was a sectarian, but unlike many others with a faith narrow and deep, she was tempered with a broad tolerance for all who walked in other ways. For years she had fed upon the spiritual food of Menno Simons, of Schwenkfeld, and of Boehme. Her chief passion was to be a saint with her heart an altar aflame before God.

She had other virtues also, and one wishes we could know her better. The celebrated but dyspeptic Samuel Pepys hints at her one-time winsomeness in describing her "a well-looked, fat, short old Dutch woman, but one that hath been heretofore pretty handsome, and I believe hath more wit than her husband."

Penn's father—Vice Admiral of the British Navy— was off to sea. Meanwhile his wife brought up her son "in the love and fear of God" at Wanstead, Essex, nurturing him upon the milk of her breasts and "the milk of the Spirit." This milk of the Spirit was that simple faith of love toward God and man which made religion a thing of the heart, and the way of life one of purity and peace. Penn's mother taught him to walk humbly before the Lord, to remember that all men are equal before God and that they should live together as brothers.

At length William's father became concerned about his son and thought it wise to wean the lad from his mother's influence and to send him to Oxford where he might be fitted properly for British society. There the young Penn chanced to hear a Quaker preacher who added to his repertoire of highly unconventional ideas. He began taking a stand against the military, he became indifferent to the established Church, he determined to have nothing to do with the courts, he refused to show deference to the King, the Bishop, and the Judge. For all men he had love; to all men he willed peace; to no man would he kowtow or so much as doff his hat.

His father was much perturbed by these outlandish ideas and actions. He determined to send the lad on a grand tour throughout the Continent in order to settle him. It didn't work out as the father planned. Everywhere young Penn went he sought out those who held similar ideas and in this way fortified his own position. In his travels he came also to know many sectarians who were filled with mystical ideas. Soon he was sharing their hopes of a golden age that would be ushered in by the Virgin Sophia, the very Wisdom of God. This coming age of peace and brotherhood—a kind of Kingdom-of-God upon earth—was symbolized by the lily or the tulip.

William Penn became a mystic. Despite his father's humiliation he joined the persecuted Quakers and began working toward that golden age of peace and brotherhood.

When at length his father died, William inherited a vast estate, much of it a debt owed him by the government. On March 4, 1681, Charles II discharged the Crown's debt by deeding to William Penn:

> A tract or part of land in America with all the islands therein . . . (providing) Two Beaver Skins bee delivered at our said Castle of Windsor, on the first day of January in every Yeare: and also the fifth part of all Golde and Silver Oare, which shall from time to time happen to bee found within the Limitts aforesaid.

Penn had already planned what he would do with this tract of land. He would make it an asylum for all, whether in England or on the Continent, who suffered persecution because of their religion. To this asylum he would invite all men everywhere who would bind themselves by conscience to live quietly in peace with God and neighbor, and he would especially encourage the hard-pressed sectarians, separatists, and mystics to find a haven and a shelter from the storm in his Pennsylvania.

Pennsylvania's origin as an asylum for those who were persecuted on account of their faith accounts for the great numbers of Dutch Saints in the southeastern section and for those who are so generously scattered throughout the length and breadth of the Commonwealth. Religion, unbelievable as it may seem, was at that time the chief promoter of persecution. Roman Catholics persecuted their Protestant neighbors; Protestants, where they were in the majority, persecuted their Catholic neighbors; Protestants persecuted one another; and the Jew was always ready bait for all. The brunt was borne by the small sectarian groups of Holland, Germany, France, Switzerland, and England. This accounts for the Mennonites, Moravians, Schwenkfelders, Amish, Brethren, Huguenots, and Quakers who have long made Pennsylvania their home. But it was too promising a venture to be monopolized by these splinter groups. The larger German communities of faith came also: Lutherans, Reformed, Roman Catholics, and Jews.

No sooner had the Pennsylvania Saints established themselves in the New World than the fruits of brotherhood began to emerge. The first constitution which was termed "The Frame of Government" gave substance and form to the Holy Experiment. It asserted:

No person, now, or at any time hereafter, Living in this Province, who shall confess and acknowledge one Almighty God to be the Creator, Upholder and Ruler of the world, And who professes, him, or herself Obliged in Conscience to Live peaceably and quietly under the civil government, shall in any case be molested or prejudiced for his, or her Conscientious persuasion or practice.

Incredible though it would seem, the very people who had been at one another's throats in the Old World became good neighbors in the New. Doubtless the very want of security in a vast wilderness inhabited by savages, the recurring plagues of sickness, the rigorous winters, the constant menace of fire, the want of shelter and often clothing and food helped stimulate a mutual concern; but beyond all this it is most evident that these Pennsylvania pioneers had the will to establish and maintain a community of brotherhood. They began and were determined to live out their lives here as good neighbors, one man putting his hand on the shoulder of another in a friendly sort of way.

Despite the many differences between the Quaker and the Pennsylvania Dutch pioneer, they worked together in promoting wholeheartedly the Holy Experiment.

When does a man stand most in need of that friendly hand upon the shoulder? When illness strikes; when fire ravages; when one man seeks to take unfair advantage of another. The Pennsylvania pioneers met this challenge by establishing in 1751 the first hospital in the New World, the Pennsylvania Hospital which functions to this day. Soon they were opening the first medical college, founding the first life insurance company, and writing the first fire insurance. Rugged individualists though they were, they believed none the less in that hand upon the shoulder.

The most colorful and yet most austere of the Pennsylvania Saints are the Amish. They are to be found in communities throughout the State, but the real home of the Amish is Lancaster County. There they possess the land, even as of old God's elect possessed the Land of Promise, a land of milk and honey. And they look the part, bearing also the names of the Old Testament patriarchs—Abraham, Isaac, Jacob, Joseph, Benjamin. The old men, with their pretentious beards, a pasty white, and with a form as rigidly controlled as the fringes on a Jewish prayer shawl, are obviously not of this world. Their hair is of the-pressed-down-pot cut variety, with bangs on the forehead, and the exact length of the hair, whether to the ear lobe, or half way down the ear, or some place in between, indicating whether they belong to the "Old Order Amish" or one of the newer and perhaps more liberal groups—more liberal by a whisker or a hair. Their clothes are all of the same cut with buttons taboo. In the mind of the Amish buttons are associated with the military. They have no radios, telephones, or electricity, and no books or magazines other than the Bible; *Der Martyrer Spiegel*, printed at Ephrata in 1748; the *Ausbund*, a hymnbook, printed by Christopher Saur at Germantown in 1751; and in exceptional cases possibly a farm magazine. They avoid, so far as possible, all social contacts with non-Amish people, and thus make themselves virtually an unapproachable caste, aloof and untouched by the world.

The Amish are Mennonites who go the second mile in the strict ways of life. Menno Simons, after whom the Mennonites are named, was born the same year Columbus discovered America. He was determined to purify the Church and in doing so established a sect of "Plain People." He set the standards high, seemingly too high, for many failed to maintain them. One of the results was that along came a bolder, stricter, harsher leader named Jacob Ammon, a Swiss Mennonite, who determined to re-reform his own people and in this way created the Amish group. The Amish have gone all out in their plain and separate way of life.

Because of religious scruples the Amish are unable to join the standard life- and fire-insurance companies. They have, nevertheless, worked out, all on their own, a most comprehensive social security. They have created a cradle-to-grave security that seldom, if ever, fails. They care for the widow and the orphan, the incapacitated and the infirm and do it in a homely, friendly way without resort to institutional means. The blows of time and chance fall upon them as upon all others, but they have a code of conduct and an agricultural pattern of family life that are never-failing shock absorbers.

A fire in the Pennsylvania Dutch country, especially if it be in an Amish section, is a memorable experience. I shall never forget how, one summer evening just as the mantle of night was silently falling upon the Lancaster County countryside, I suddenly heard dinner bells frantically announcing, "'s a Feia, 's a Feia, 's a Feia!" Soon all about me were the pounding feet of frenzied horses; every lane and byway was jammed with buggies and wagons, with men, women, and children running, even long-skirted mothers with tiny babies in their arms, all bent upon getting to the fire.

The fire engine from Blue Ball drew up behind, gonging its way through the mad crowd, but already the flames were winging high above Jake Beiler's barn. The pathetic whinny of the horses, the awful moaning of the cows overwhelmed the surrounding clamor. Men were dashing to open the stable doors to persuade, pull, drive or kick the cows and the horses beyond the entrapping flames. Others were salvaging farm machinery. Their task was lightened because it was Saturday night and the barn had been readied for Church services with the threshing floor swept and polished and all the benches in place.

The flames mounted higher and higher. Each moment was more desperate than the last. Then it was that I heard some one call out, "Parre Stoltzfoos iss cum!"

Parre Stoltzfoos is a name the Amish pronounce with reverence. If there is trouble, hardship, or sorrow, he is the first to help; if joy, he is first to share it with others; in evil times and good times the word that is first upon the lips and first in the hearts of his people is "Parre Stoltzfoos."

The Amish have three grades of clergy based doubtless upon the ancient order of bishop, priest, and deacon. The "Volle Diener" is the Bishop who has general oversight and to whom is reserved the sacramental ministry of ordination by the laying on of hands, the celebration of the Holy Communion, and the performance of the marriage ceremony. He has helpers in the "Diener zum Buch," who are set apart primarily to preach "venever der turn cums" and also to assist with the Holy Communion. As a rule each congregation has two "Diener zum Buch." Then there is the "Armen Diener," or deacon, who has oversight over the charities of the congregation.

Parre Stoltzfoos was the "Volle Diener," and as Bishop he might have stood aside while Deacon Huyard assumed the tasks of danger at the fire. But Bishop Stoltzfoos was not one who could hold aloof, for he ever remembered how the Scripture made plain that he who would be first must be servant of all. Instantly he pitched in with a will. He gave a hand to salvaging the machinery, putting his strong, broad shoulders to the wheel of the wagon and the wheel of the threshing machine—lifting, heaving, grunting, sweating. When others failed to rescue the prize bull—the most valuable animal on the farm—Bishop Stoltzfoos made one last effort and escaped as by a miracle, for the huge timbers gave way over his head and tons of burning hay catapulted into the stables. He emerged, a man who had come through fire.

By this time sparks began falling upon the house. Miraculously, under the direction of Andrew Yoder, men began to appear on the house roof with buckets in their hands. The women formed a bucket brigade, emptying in no time the water trough, the milk cooling tank, exhausting the spring and threatening the well. The barn roof caved in with a mighty thud while a canopy of mounting flames and falling embers covered all. A little

11

later the barn walls began to crumble; hours later there was nothing left of Jake Beiler's barn but hot stone walls and a mouldering stench—stubborn timbers burning, the smell of mingled dung and carcasses taking possession of the night air. I stayed until Jake broke down and cried like a baby. Someone was urging him to take a shot of "Schnaps," but he refused. Jake leaned against the grape arbor—I thought of Jonah under the vine and wanting to die. A man stepped forward and put his hand upon Jake's shoulder. It was Bishop Stoltzfoos.

The day after the fire Bishop Stoltzfoos and Dave Glick, the carpenter, were at Jake's farm when the sun came up over the eastern hills. By noon the drawings for the new barn were completed, and the time of the barn-raising was agreed upon. Parre Stoltzfoos would announce it at the "G-may," the next Church meeting. A month later a new and improved barn stood on the foundations of the old, a cooperative venture of the entire Amish community. The labor was free as were most of the logs and the lumber. Moreover, the loss of cattle and horses was compensated by neighbors who came forward with gifts in kind. With the Amish, that hand upon the shoulder works miracles.

Far across the State, in a section where no Amish live, there is a one-room country school named Red Brush. It is just what its name implies. About it live the Workleys, Peffers, Dindingers, Schweinegrubers, Moyers, and Gettmans in sufficient numbers to constitute a considerable degree of Dutch leaven. Years ago, each autumn when the dogwood cast its leaves and the red berries showed their glory in the November sun, the berry-laden branches were brought into the school, stripped of their fruit, and with needles and thread long garlands were made which were then looped and draped about the room by way of creating a festive atmosphere for Thanksgiving and for Christmas.

Once, as the berries were being strung, a needle bypassed and plowed into the thumb of a little girl whose ancestors had escaped from slavery into free Pennsylvania a century earlier. Whereupon one of the older girls exclaimed, "Why, Rose Jones, your blood's the same color as ours!" The Pennsylvania Dutch have long known that God made of one blood all Roman Catholics, Orthodox, Protestants, and Jews. And, happily, they are not always so retarded as at Red Brush in discovering that all men are of one blood.

Insistence upon the equality of all men before God, despite racial or sectarian differences, was proclaimed by one of the Saints' most gifted leaders in the days of William Penn. He was the learned and pious Francis Daniel Pastorius who, while living in his hermit's cave by the Wissahickon, put himself and his people on record in the year 1688 as unconditionally opposed to slavery. In his protest, the first in the Western Hemisphere, he was joined by Dirck op den Graeff, Abraham op den Graeff and Gerhard Hendriks. Many years later this brave declaration of Pastorius was to be underwritten on a Pennsylvania battlefield by the gallant soldiers of Gettysburg, who sealed and ratified it with their own blood.

When one considers the achievement of brotherhood among our Pennsylvania Dutch, the story of the village of Bally is sure to warm the heart. St. Paul's at Goshen-hoppen, now called Bally, was the third Roman Catholic Church to be established in the Commonwealth. When the Reverend Theodore Schneider, S. J., arrived in 1741 he found in the community one Church, a log structure used by the Mennonites. The good priest had scarcely made himself known when the entire community banded together and Mennonite and Moravian joined the Roman Catholics in taking to the woods with their axes to fell trees, shape the timbers, and at a community raising to dedicate St. Paul's Church to the glory of God and the happiness of all his children.

This spirit of brotherhood, bridging many a divisive chasm, still prevails in Bally. Community-wide cooperation between Roman Catholics and Protestants continues unabated and, moreover, in Bally there is the balm of healing for Protestant divisiveness as well. The little Mennonite Church now has a Schwenkfelder for its pastor. Besides his parochial duties he has found time to distinguish himself as a theological professor, teaching not in a Mennonite or Schwenkfelder school, but in a New England institution of Congregational origin.

There is another Pennsylvania community that has magnified itself in the friendly way of life. It is the village of Aaronsburg, Center County, in the beautiful State University region. This community was settled by a group of Pennsylvania Dutch with the Lutherans predominating. I remember Aaronsburg as a clean, quiet town with tall trees. Some day I'm going to take a closer look at the town, its Lutheran Church and graveyard, and all the tombstones with the Pennsylvania Dutch names.

Chances are there's a Virgin Sophia and some tulips emblazoned on those old head stones.

I also want to learn more about Aaron Levy, the pious Jew, who gave the land for the Church, graveyard and school. His neighbors were kind to him and he in turn reciprocated in a magnificent way. Here was a Pennsylvania pioneer whose people had known imprisonment in the ghettos of the Old World. Aaron Levy could easily have justified himself in living apart, nursing suspicion and bitterness in his heart. But such a life was not for him. He went the second mile as a good neighbor should. In doing so he earned for Aaronsburg an achievement in brotherhood, and through his generosity toward the Christian Church he bespeaks the coming day when Jew and Gentile will better appreciate their common spiritual heritage and will walk together as children of one Heavenly Father.

Wherever one goes in Pennsylvania, whether to Philadelphia, Germantown, Bally, Aaronsburg or to Dutch communities in Western Pennsylvania, one finds life expressed in terms of that hand upon the shoulder. In rural areas it means your neighbor's door is open and he stands ready to help. In the villages it means a friendly welcome not unlike the kind Hattie Brunner gives to those who find her door in Rheinholds. Perhaps you have heard of her famous antique place and of the celebrated people who frequent it, some of them coming from Hollywood, some of them with names like DuPont. Before rapping at her door you may feel obliged to screw up your courage. I must confess I did. You rap and presently there's a woman, Dutch as they come, with a big gingham apron and a smile that's equally broad. She flings out her arms like a woman gathering in clothes from the line. "Ach vell," she says, "chust cum right in un make yourself to home. Take off your sings; make yourself down. Dere's der Bretzels un der Ebbels. Excuse me, I'm on der phone yet vonct."

You nibble at the pretzels, still a little fearful of the pressure she may put on you to buy that grandfather's clock with the moon face, or some of the Stiegel glass high in the cupboard, or some of the colorful fraktur on the walls, or, perhaps, that slant-top desk in bird's-eye maple with dogwood pulls. But Hattie is not one to high-pressure anyone. Soon you are at her table. The coffee is hot and you find that the home-baked "Schnitz" pie, dried-apple pie as the English call it, goes well with vanilla ice cream. You talk about the Dutch stuff that collectors like, such as the tulip ware, but Hattie prefers the more personal subjects such as singing in the Church choir, or the lump on her breast that has been giving her concern despite the doctor's reassurance. You look all around. You see everything. You buy nothing. You overstay your time. When you manage to escape, you hear Hattie calling after you, "Cum again, quick," as she waves a friendly goodbye.

There was a time when this open-door, open-heart attitude of the Pennsylvania Saints was occasionally taken advantage of in an unfair way. Tramps begging for shelter and food knew that they would not be turned away. Often by virtue of a solemn promise to chop wood afterward, they enjoyed a breakfast of bacon and eggs, sausage and fried potatoes, shoofly pie, funnycake, cheesecake, coffee, and cookies. All too often after breakfast the well-fed tramp walked around the woodshed and disappeared. A day or two later there would be another uninvited guest and the breakfast-woodchopping bargain would be repeated. So likewise the escape.

There were, however, those weary travellers who paid off in an appropriate way. They were the professional penmen and fraktur artists who went from farmhouse to farmhouse filling in, with expert hand and carefully chosen color, the family register in the old leather-bound "Heilige Schrift," listing the births, the deaths, the marriages, giving in each instance the hour of the day or night, and the sign of the Zodiac. Sometimes they were called upon to make "Taufschein"—Baptismal Certificates; or "Haus Segen"—House Blessings, illuminating them with rich-colored tulips, symbols of the friendly way of life.

Long years ago a weary traveler spent a night in the home of my grandfather. Granddad was a cobbler by night, a farmer by day. That is easily explained by simply stating there were sixteen children, beginning with Jake, ending with Anna; with Frank, my father, in between. The old farmhouse on Scholar's Run was of generous proportions, but, figure it anyway you can, it must have been jammed to the eaves. The situation afforded ample grounds for turning away strangers who desired to spend the night. But the Brenners couldn't say "no."

One evening as the family circle formed by the open fire it included a newcomer of talent and grace, who managed in a few short hours to make a contribution toward the enrichment of life that the Brenner family has never forgotten. Next morning, before his departure, he asked for a sheet of paper and began writing upon it upside down. That paper, with its excellency in penmanship, is on the desk before me. It is written in German, English and Hebrew and reads:

> Bro. Jacob Brenner
> & Wife (nee Elizabeth Goehring):
> I thank you with all my heart for your great kindness and hospitality you have bestowed upon me last night and this morning.
> I am not worthy of the least of all the mercies and of all the truth which Thou hast shewed unto thy servant—Genesis 32:10.
> *Written Upside Down*

. . ."chust another hand upon the shoulder."

2—"She Feels To Teach"

A sgraffeta dish begotten in the Pennsylvania Dutch country depicts a young girl, in Mennonite dress and a generous bonnet, conversing with a younger girl, Mennonite also. About the edge of the plate are these words, "She Feels to Teach."

I often get to thinking about that girl and wishing that I knew the story of her life. Was she, perhaps, the wallflower type who couldn't catch a man, and in her desperation veered toward the monastic way and consented to be a "Schulmeisterin"—a schoolmaster that wears skirts? Was she, perhaps, a so-called delicate girl for whom it would be hard to milk cows, pitch hay, dig potatoes, and produce babies; consequently, "She Feels to Teach"? Was she, perhaps, an especially gifted girl who was conscious of her possibilities and who, bowing to the dictates of conscience, felt constrained to teach? Whatever the motivation and the circumstances, here was a girl, a Mennonite girl for whom the teaching profession would be difficult to enter, who, nevertheless, joined the ranks of those who have found nothing better to do than to teach school.

On every hand one hears that school teaching is not easy. It is pretty generally known that it's not a glamour job, nor does it pay off in excessive cash. There are, however, certain rewards and above all an abiding satisfaction such as is true of every vocation that contributes generously to the betterment of mankind.

In the days of the Pennsylvania Dutch pioneers, there were in each community three men who towered above all others in public esteem. They were the "Parre," the "Schulmeister," and the "Dokter." The Schulmeister was in all ways closely associated with the Parre. He shared in the work of catechizing and if the Parre became ill, it was usually the Schulmeister who was called upon to carry on—to read the Scriptures, the prayers, the sermon, and, if need be, to bury the dead. The teacher shared the responsibilities of the pastor in promoting throughout the community the ideals and techniques of the better life, yes, even the saintly life to which these pioneers believed themselves called.

The Pennsylvania Dutch pioneers reverenced the pastor, the doctor, and the teacher. It must be confessed, however, that they also had their difficulties with the school teachers, the schools, and with the learning process itself. Their chief complaint they put in these words: "I get too soon olt un too late schmart."

At first this difficulty centered in the language problem. They were, despite the name Dutch, a people of German origin and a German-speaking people who made use of a dialectical form of the mother tongue. When the first of them came to Pennsylvania the British officials asked about their language. They answered in good German that they spoke "Deutsch." The officials didn't fully understand. It was a hard word for English tongues; the edge soon wore off and it became just plain "Dutch"— whence the name Pennsylvania Dutch.

These people came in such great numbers that soon it was a question whether the official language of the state would be German or English. The Dutch had the votes on their side. But they also had wise leaders such as the Muhlenbergs, who knew that Pennsylvania could not stand alone—English it would have to be.

That decision, however, did not change the language of the Dutch country, and on the farm and in the home it was the kind of German commonly called "Dutch" that prevailed. This language was, and still is, in some sections used almost exclusively.

The Plain People are much given to Dutch. The Amish talk nothing but Dutch among themselves. Even the so-called gay Dutch are slow to forget it. A few years ago when one walked into an Allentown store he was sure to be greeted in Dutch; it was also the language of the barroom, the barbershop, the blacksmith shop, and even in the Church the sermon might be in Dutch. This made it difficult for the younger ones when they began public school. On the first day of school the bell rang and the barefoot kids funneled into the one-room school, only to discover that the "tietscher" spoke a foreign tongue. My dad told me the first day he went to Red Brush School he didn't know an English word—and my people were far out in the western part of the state, beyond even the fringes of the typical Dutch country.

The Pennsylvania Dutch country is bounded on the east and west by two great rivers, the Delaware and the Susquehanna. On the south it spills over the Mason-Dixon Line, while on the north it juts into the Pocono Mountains and beyond.

The Dutch are by nature farmers; no one surpasses them in the cultivation of the soil. Being by nature farmers, they have the knack of spotting and acquiring the best land. They were first to know the virtues of lime and today wherever in the State there is limestone beneath the soil there is the likelihood that you will find a Dutchman astride it.

These Dutch pioneers had a special liking for the valleys where the soil is deep, the water plentiful, and the pastures green. They first possessed the banks of the Wissahickon close by Philadelphia, then they took over the banks of the Schuylkill, then they fanned out into the beautiful Perkiomen Valley and the Conestoga, and on beyond the Dutchland itself into the broad Cumberland Valley.

Finally the winds carried the Dutch pollen farther west, creating islands of Dutch culture in such communities as Somerset, Berlin, Greenville, Zelienople and Harmony, and on into Ohio.

Whether in the heart of the Dutchland or beyond, these people have always maintained a wholesome skepticism about the matter of education. Many of them hold that the chief purpose of life is work, hard work. In order to do this necessary work effectively, they realize a knowledge of the three, or counting religion, the four Rs is necessary, so they have always been unanimous and enthusiastic about elementary education. But the so-called higher education has not won their universal support.

The Dutch are of two kinds: plain and fancy. The plain Dutch are easy to spot. They wear a peculiar garb. Usually the women have their heads covered with white prayer caps and their middles with aprons, while the men spurn all the fancy trimmings such as neckties and even buttons and wear odd hats and beards. They are for education at the bottom, but they don't go in for college degrees.

The Mennonites and Amish constitute the bulk of the Plain People. Mennonites, while rather skeptical of the so-called higher education, are not of one mind about it. They have their own colleges and many of their leaders are learned men who have distinguished themselves in college or university. With the Amish it is different. They are farmers pure and simple, and they are going to remain such. They want to know how to read and write and how at last to make their way to heaven's gate and that's about all. Latin or algebra, or philosophy? Not for the Amish. "It makes fer faul (lazy), 's is' net gudt fer farming, ain't?"

The gay Dutch, and that's 90 percent of them, are more difficult to spot. They have no peculiar garb and if they speak the best of English, which many of them do, you will never know they are Dutch until you get down deep in their hearts. I was one of the gay Dutch, and so far as education is concerned I was fortunate to escape the inhibitions that shackle my plain cousins. Even in my pre-school days Grandmother had me marked out for a Parre or something of that nature. Her reasoning was simple and conclusive. More than once I heard her bemoan, "You are too slow un doppich fer work on der farm."

Consequently, so far as I was aware of anything, I trudged the long way to school the very first day with high ideals and the goal of a higher education in my mind. I was given a Brumbaugh Primer—and there could have been no more propitious beginning, for the Brumbaughs were Pennsylvania Dutch and "Saints" as well—and made a member of a class whose first assignment was to learn how to count to a hundred.

In order to augment our progress, penny post cards, the picture kind, some of them heavily adorned with tinsel or other showy "gingerbread," had been procured by the teacher. These were to be our reward. The first member of the class to master the assignment would get the pick of "all of the pretty picture cards."

I aimed for the first card; my aim was bad. One after another mastered the difficult technique, counted to a hundred and claimed his "Oscar." I always got stuck in the mud at thirty—I just couldn't remember what came after twenty-nine. After the teacher prompted me on the thirty I could breeze right along to a hundred. But neither prayers nor tears availed to get me over that thirty hump.

I suppose I would still be stuck at twenty-nine had not Aunt Avis come to my rescue. "Think of your dirty face, Scott; then switch that dirty into thirty, and there you have it."

The next day I remembered my dirty face and reached the goal. Instead of being first, I was last. There was no picking of an "Oscar" for me; the card that everyone had rejected, that was mine.

I feel differently about it now, for from time to time I look at that card and I know it was always meant for me. It is like a tailor-made suit; it fits. The card features an old straw hat, the kind farmer boys once wore, generous in dimensions and sadly torn. As the card pictures it, that hat is diverted from its original purpose and has become a cosy hang-out for a litter of black and white fox terrier puppies. Inside the hat are four mischievous pups, filling it to the brim. Outside is one other, a sad-eyed puppy who is obliged to content himself with a look-in, for he has come too late. The card underscores the tragedy with two pointed words: "Just arrived."

There was a time in the early days of the Commonwealth when the public school hardly existed in the Dutch country. For the most part the early schools were Church inspired and Church supervised. In those days there was little or no effort to introduce the English language—even the textbooks were in German. One of my library shelves is filled with these *Deutsch Reformirtes* and *Hoch-Deutsches Lutherisches A-B-C Und Namen-Buchlein fuer Kinder*. In many respects these little German books are remarkably advanced in teaching methods. Despite the limited printing facilities of that time, much use was made of pictures.

One of these books, and I have many like it, illustrates the alphabet in an interesting way. Beside the letter "A" are the words "Apfel" and "Affe" and the picture of an apple—Could it be an apple for the teacher?—and an ape. It is likely that there were some apes in school, but this was the imported variety direct from the jungle. The ape is juggling the apple and underneath is this verse:

> *Den Affen sieht das Kind und Lacht*
> *Wie er beim Apfel Possen macht.*

> The ape saw the child and laughed
> For he would do the apple trick.

The letter "H" comes into its own with the words "Hund" and "Hahn"—the picture of a dog and a rooster.

The rhyme limps along:

Oft kraeht der Hahn nach Mitternacht,
Wo uns der treue Hund bewacht.

After midnight the rooster oft crows
In order to awaken the faithful dog.

For some reason the Pennsylvania Saints have always been partial to roosters. The robin; the "distlefink" or wild canary; the parakeet, once a native of these parts; the peacock, and the rooster—these are the feathered friends that caught the eye of the Pennsylvania Dutch pioneers and these are the birds they depict in their folk art.

Nearly everyone appreciates the rooster when he is served at the holiday table. The Dutch would yield to no one in this. But why did they put the rooster on so many of their Church steeples? Was it because of the Apostle Peter and the crowing of the cock that night when he betrayed his Lord? There is, fortunately, one sure reason why the Saints exalted the rooster and the school books bear incontrovertible evidence. Sometimes the covers depict David and his harp; sometimes Martin Luther in his ecclesiastical garb. George Washington, "Vater seines Vaterland," made at least one cover. It is, however, the rooster, there can be no question about it, that takes first place in the pin-up gallery. Usually it is a pompous, cocky rooster that adorns the back cover. He is perched on the fence with a graceful curvature of the neck, a wide-opened eye, and a fluffing of the feathers that suggests that he's pumping up the bellows on the inside and is about to give vent to his penetrating alarm:

Der Hahn weckt uns des Morgens frueh
Mit seinem Kickericki.

The rooster wakes us early in the morning
With his cock-a-doodle-doo.

That is the great virtue of the rooster—he starts his day early and does his best to arouse every sleepyhead. Perhaps his dominant position on the school book was a help with sleepy boys and girls.

After the A-B-C books the lessons became more advanced, filled with precepts and admonitions that are difficult for the most mature to practice in life's school. There are lines of immediate import; such as:

Do not play in school nor tease those who sit
   next to you;
For this is wrong even if the teacher does not
   see it.

A more difficult assignment is put in verse:

Whatever brawls disturb the street,
There should be peace at home;
Where sisters dwell and brothers meet,
Quarrels should never come.
Birds in their little nests agree
And 'tis a shameful sight
When children of one family
Fall out and chide and fight.

The curriculum of the school in those days contained one course no longer taught, namely, the art of fraktur. Fraktur is essentially an advanced type of penmanship making use of Gothic letters. Thus the Pennsylvania

Dutch continued to practice an art that was perfected in the Middle Ages and seen at its best in ancient illuminated manuscripts. The artistry of the Dutch Saints, as they practiced it in the schools, is not comparable with that of the old-time monks, but, on the other hand, its very primitive quality endows it with unique charm.

The Pennsylvania Dutch school teacher was obliged to spend many hours designating fraktur patterns called "vorschrifts," to be copied by the boys and girls. Sometimes the teacher's help was needed in shaping the quill and in mixing the home-brewed colors which each pupil was required to supply together with a "coloring box." Despite the severe limitations in coloring media and in paper, these pioneer schools of the Saints trained many in the artistry of design and color as the numerous frakturs in the homes of the Dutch bear ample testimony to this day.

I have an "A-B-C Buch" done entirely in fraktur by a school boy named Henry Diehl. One cannot conceive a more artistic design of letters. Each letter is colorful, ornate, and unique—breathing a blessing peculiarly its own. The colors are blue, red, brown, yellow and green. The years, far from detracting from their glory, have softened and blended them so that they are like the last, soft moments of a glorious sunset. Each letter has its tulips—some letters are almost obscured with a profusion of flowers. Many are populated by curious snail-like creatures, while in a few instances a human face protrudes. Henry Diehl, the Saint and the artist, is more deserving of adulation than these lines can ever suggest. It is obvious that the Saint and the artist in him were more or less in conflict making hard the way of his soul. If his conscience still troubles him, may he henceforth rest in peace. After he had perfected his A-B-Cs he appended this confession:

> The A-B-C's are at an end. It also means that the time that was used is like an eye turned away from eternity. Shun the earthly and prepare thyself for the heavenly.

Henry Diehl must have been a saint in the real sense of the word. There have been Pennsylvania Saints who have not held up too well under adverse weather conditions. They have been like the angels that once hung on my Christmas tree—they became soiled. I put them under the water faucet. The wings came loose and the gilded halo faded. Nevertheless, I still like them and so far as I'm concerned they are angels still.

I remember Howard, a Pennsylvania Dutch boy from the beautiful Cumberland Valley. The Valley has played a big part in the life of the Saints. Here it was that the Pennsylvania Dutch poet Henry Harbaugh was born. Here the schoolhouse stood that he has memorialized in the Dutch poem "Das Alt Schulhaus an der Krick" Henry Harbaugh concluded his poem with this petition:

> *Heit is 's 'xaectly zwansig Johr,*
> *Dass ich bin owwe naus;*
> *Nau bin ich widder lewig z'rick*
> *Un schteh am Schulhaus an d'r Krick,*
> *Juscht neekscht an's Dady's Haus.*

> Today it is just twenty years,
> Since I began to roam;

Now, safely back, I stand once more,
Before the quaint old school-house door,
Close by my father's home.
I've been in many houses since,
   Of marble built, and brick;
Though grander far, their aim they miss,
To lure my heart's old love from this
   Old school-house at the creek.

    . . . . .

Oh horcht, ihr Leit, wu nooch mir lebt,
   Ich schreib eich noch des Schtick:
Ich warn eich, droh eich, gebt doch Acht,
Un nemmt uf immer gut enacht,
Des Schulhaus an der Krick!

Ye, who shall live when I am dead—
Write down my wishes quick—
Protect it, love it, let it stand, '
A way-mark in this changing land—
That school-house at the creek.

Well, the schoolhouse at the creek is gone, but in its
place there is a more enduring institution founded by the
Pennsylvania Dutch and by Henry Harbaugh in particular—Mercersburg Academy.

Howard's home was in this same Cumberland Valley,
but he chose to get his "higher" education on the banks
of the Perkiomen. At the appointed time he reported to
a Pennsylvania Dutch college intent upon becoming a
Parre. Since I was to be his "big brother" I had been
given in advance some information about him and the
probable time of his arrival. It was my job to welcome

him to the college and safely steer him into the way of his exalted profession.

My heart sank when I saw him moseying in his gawky way up the path to Bomberger Hall. He was a freshman all right, my "little brother." A farmer's hat was on his head; in one hand he carried an umbrella; under the other arm a huge Victorian Bible—the kind with the big metal clasps, and the heavy pages cut out and shaped for the family album, and the register for marriages, births, and deaths.

Howard stuck his umbrella in the ground as the farmer would his pitchfork and we shook hands—Howard insisted that the shake be hard and long. He smelled of the barnyard and of prayers. Piety virtually oozed in his grasp. I was fearful lest he suggest that we kneel down and pray on the spot. He called me "Brother," and that was hardly to a sophomore's liking. I concealed my dislike as best I could and showed him to his room. His Bible I took and put on the upper shelf in the closet, pushing it far back out of sight. I decided to be straightforward with him and bluntly announced, "You won't need your Bible—not in college, Howard." I wanted to put his hat in the wastebasket, but I lost my nerve. That could be taken care of at a later date. The umbrella, as I knew, was also of rather questionable value, for most any college guy would brave the heaviest rain rather than bother with an umbrella, and yet it didn't seem quite cricket to dispose of all his worldly goods at one fell swoop. It would take time for Howard to get into the groove.

My first responsibility—there was not the shadow of

a doubt about it—was to dehydrate Howard of the superfluous piety that had managed to waterlog him. I went to work at once, and my success was phenomenal. Within a few weeks Howard had succeeded in shedding his piety as a snake sheds its skin in the spring. So far as popularity was concerned, it wasn't long until he made the hit parade. He proved himself a shark at cards and it was evident that he was learning about women, too.

Howard also joined the Slifer gang and became an active member of the water-dowsing crew that threatened to turn Freeland Hall into Freeland Lake. Somehow a number of the boys managed to get master keys. Then in the early morning hours, when the winter winds whipped the thermometer to zero, the water dowsers went to work. They took the huge garbage cans that served as waste collectors and filled them with as much water as a brawny fullback or tackle could manage, and then quietly invading the predestined rooms, unleashed a Niagara of ice-cold water upon those who were deep in their dreams and their blankets. The bleary-eyed victims were helpless as they threshed about in the water. The blankets; and the bed, first covered with water and then ice, were knocked out of commission for nights to come. You can dry your skin, but it takes time to dry a mattress —this I learned at college.

Howard's progress in higher education was too rapid and it wasn't long until he merited the attention of the Student Council and of the College Dean. He suffered the usual penalties: free advice and a few demerits. Having come through the fire without too much singeing, it wasn't long until he again stood before the august tribunal. This time the demerits were considerable and just short of expulsion. Moreover, the Dean was obliged to write a letter to Howard's family, informing them of the number of demerits that had been visited upon their pious son.

By this time I was much worried on Howard's account, and repented myself of the spiritual debunking which I had so successfully promoted. I was giving serious thought to fishing that Bible from its hiding place in the closet and I was determined to give Howard a straightforward dressing-down.

I summoned him to my room and dished it out as best I could, but I saw that I was not making much progress. In one last desperate effort I resorted to dragging out his family and his home ties.

"What," I demanded, "will your parents think when they get the Dean's letter, and they learn about all your demerits?"

Howard smiled. Quick as a flash he answered, "What will they think about those demerits? Demerits—they'll be happy as hell—they'll figure the college has conferred an honor upon me."

Well, the years have gone by and I am sure that Howard has long since regained much of his inherent piety. He is, I am told, a good Parre down in the Pennsylvania Dutch country and is beloved of his people. He should be. He has many virtues and abilities including the art of mimicry. If he ever got on television, he would become a household god. But I venture that Howard is most helpful in counseling with young people who are intent upon college, and just in case some of them should get in trouble on the campus, I can recommend him as one who knows the way out.

Education is a great thing for those who drink it in. Education is at its best when it is a shared experience between the teacher and the pupil. It is also a virtue for those who specialize in giving it out, and we must be everlastingly grateful to all who "feel to teach." There have been able students among the Pennsylvania Saints, and great teachers, too. Perhaps the greatest was Christopher Dock.

I had never heard of Christopher Dock—it's amazing what the schools fail to teach us—until one day in a Dutch attic I picked up a mildewed booklet: *Schul-Ordnung, (School Management), Christopher Dock . . . Germantown, Gedruckt und zu finden bey Christop Saur, 1770.* Along with it were two other pamphlets by the same publisher and author. All three proved interesting. Here was a pioneer school teacher, who began teaching about 1710, setting forth his objectives and methods. His overall objective was the good life envisioned in William Penn's "Holy Experiment"; his methods were his own and were wrought out in response to the demands of the American frontier. As I read along in his book I came upon observations such as these:

"Accustom yourself to waken at the right time. (There were no alarm clocks then.) . . . Wash your face and hands without splashing. (I know mothers who wish they had kept this in the course.) . . . Rinse your mouth and rub your teeth with your fingers" (and that in a day when there was no toothbrush nor paste.) When it comes to meals he said, "Be satisfied with what is given you . . .

don't throw the bones under the table . . . don't speak unless spoken to . . . don't put the leftovers in your pocket." When at Church, "Bow at the mention of God's name . . . listen to the sermon . . . memorize the text . . . don't talk in Church; if you get sleepy stand awhile. Avoid scratching the head, chewing the fingers, restlessness; remember you are a child of God and you shall not always live in this world; pray God to make your end good."

What I read prodded me to find out more about the "pious schoolmaster of the Skippack." I learned that he began teaching at Skippack and that he also had a large farm nearby. He worked the farm and taught, first at one school, and finally at three. His schools were at Skippack, at Salford, and also at Germantown, where Christopher Sauer, the Bible printer, sent his son.

In traveling from school to school Dock rode a horse, keeping an alert eye upon the woods for any Indian that might be lurking in the neighborhood. Farmer and teacher, he was also a mail-carrier. This he did in order to hasten the mastery of the "Rs." He had his boys in Germantown write the girls in Skippack, and the girls in Skippack, the boys in Salford. As he made his rounds and opened his mail bag he was reasonably sure he could count upon the inquisitive cooperation of his scholars, for he was utilizing the best of pedagogical techniques and cashing in, as well, on a little sex appeal. Sometimes, as apparently the good teacher knew, a dash of sex goes a long way in stimulating the learning process.

He was interested not only in the boys and girls within the four walls of his schools, but also in their homes, their parents, and in their family life. Through his boys and girls he would have the pollen of culture brush off on their elders. Whenever a student did something worthy of note, the schoolmaster took out his quill, his box of homemade colors, and designed a fraktur beautiful with tulips and birds and the name of that boy or girl. On the other side he would specify the achievement which he deemed worthy of praise and would conclude his note to the parents in words of this nature: "John is hereby entitled to all reasonable deference and honor, and also to two fried eggs and a slab of bacon for breakfast." Little wonder that he turned out men and women worthy of the Holy Experiment.

Christopher Dock had a practical bent, too, as his words in the *"Schul-Ordnung"* make clear:

> It is also to be noted that children find it necessary to leave the room, and one must permit them to do so . . . But the clamor to go-out would continue all day, and sometimes without need, so that occasionally two or three are out at the same time, playing. To prevent this I have driven a nail in the door-post, on which hangs a wooden tag. Any one needing to leave the room looks for the tag. If it is on the nail this is his permit to go out without asking.

I must add that if the tag were not upon the doorpost it was not so easy to get out. The schoolmaster demanded some evidence of urgency and doubtless there were times when he miscalculated, as other teachers have been known to do, much to their own inconvenience.

As the title "pious" indicates, there was spiritual depth to Christopher Dock. The culture he was concerned about was to be shot through with Christian morality. One day the pious schoolmaster tarried at the Skippack School long after the accustomed hour. Several of the boys set out to investigate, and peering discretely through the windows, saw their teacher, enfolded in the shadows of the eventide, kneeling at his desk in prayer. They were not surprised. Often he had paused in the midst of a lesson to lift by name some boy or girl on the wings of prayer. They knew, too, that it was his custom to close each school day kneeling in prayer, with the school roll, containing the names of all, spread out on his desk before him. In a sense his children were the pearly beads of his rosary, and as he named them one by one it was that they might grow in the favor of God and their fellow-men, and come, finally, to a good end.

The boys waited; the master tarried. Finally, they tip-toed to his side only to discover that their beloved teacher, praying for his boys and girls, had answered "Present" to his own final roll call.

The culture of the Dutch Saints is broad and deep, but nowhere is it more glorious than in the life and labors of Christopher Dock. I think of the pious schoolmaster of the Skippack and there is within me the urge to salute everyone who "feels to teach."

3—The Birds Sing Best In Pennsylvania

MAN WHO had traveled widely and at one time put down his roots in the far West, and later transplanted himself to the sunny South, each time saying to himself, "This is the place," came back, at last, to Pennsylvania. Where he had been born he bought a farm, a stone house, and a Dutch barn with barn signs included, and made it his home ever after.

One day I asked him why he came back. He drove his spade deep into the rich earth, pushed his cap back from his forehead, and answered, "The birds sing best in Pennsylvania."

Even as he spoke the shrill crescendo of a flicker in the distant woodlot pierced my ears and the sweet, rapturous melody of a song sparrow sounded like a pean of praise for the Pennsylvania Dutch. I was not fully satisfied with his statement and I asked him, "Dan, what are you getting at when you say the birds sing best in Pennsylvania?"

"Oh, shucks," he answered. "I guess it's more than the birds; you know what I mean."

"No, Dan, I don't."

"Well, it's this way; there's something solid about this Pennsylvania Dutch country. Take this farm, for five generations the Keelys have lived here. Why they ever let it get out of the family, I'll never know; my luck that they did. Why, when I moved in they even turned over the original deed—William Penn signature, the Great Seal, the whole works."

"Your luck was sure with you that day, Dan."

"Know why I treasure that old deed? It tells me that people stay put here. Like that oak, families root here.

I've decided that when they say the last words over me I'm going to have them carry me down to the meadow there and dig me in at the old Keely graveyard. Once I get the old stone wall repaired and some of the blackberry bushes rooted out, there'll be room. If I live here and die here, why not be buried here?"

I fully agreed, for I had long since come to like these cozy, homey, family burial plots with their stone walls plastered white and their tombstones embossed with tulips and the Virgin Sophia. To moulder in the very soil you tilled, the soil your children and children's children will till—but I thought it better to change the subject. So I asked, "What about the old Dutch stuff in the house when you took over?"

"Oh, there wasn't very much. Found an old Pennsylvania rifle in the attic."

"An honest-to-goodness old one?"

"Old as they come. Wouldn't be surprised if it had been left here when Washington and his men dug in at Valley Forge—he had his headquarters in that house for a couple of days, you know. Oh yes, there was a Bible there, too. You'd be interested in seeing it. One of the Saur Bibles; I think it was the 1763 edition. You see what I mean when I say, 'The birds sing best in Pennsylvania'?"

"I understand; why don't we come right out with it? The birds sing best in Dutch Pennsylvania."

The Pennsylvania Dutch country is rich with history and culture. These Dutch Saints, as I like to name them, have made life good, discovered meaning in its mystery and made music of its discords. Dan was not alone in sensing this. I, too, had made the discovery. As the youth-

ful pastor of a parish not far from Valley Forge, closer Skippack, and not too distant from Germantown or Ephrata, I had for some time sensed the hallmarks of Dutch culture all about me.

In putting together the cultural pattern of our Pennsylvania Saints I had a kindly mentor in an elderly neighbor, Frederick Hillbiber, who was steeped in the natural sciences and in historical lore, especially Pennsylvania history. His Schwenksville home was a kind of museum— a magnificent library, unique mineral collection, and antiques everywhere.

He told me how for many years he had collected Americana, chiefly old books. Once he stumbled upon the rarest of Franklin almanacs in trash about to be burned. He found "Richard Saunders" most interesting, but some years later, in a weak moment, he sold that almanac for a munificent sum. The truth is my neighbor was so successful in his antiquarian pursuits that his house began giving way under the weight of the vast collection and he was obliged to call in carpenters to prop it up.

One day he said to me, "Scott, you're a young man and you've got a car. Why don't you get interested in these old things—you know my books and stuff?"

"I'm interested," I said, "but where does that get me?"

"That's what I've been thinking about. Why don't we form a kind of corporation? You're the pastor—you've got entree. All you need to do is get your foot in the door; then we'll talk our way into the attic—I know what's good."

"Oh, I don't know, Frederick. Afraid I don't have the time."

"Young man, you've got the time; take it. We can do it in your off hours. Let's get the car out tomorrow. We'll visit these old Dutch houses up and down the Perkiomen—might find a Saur Bible, or even an Aitken; and there could be William Penn deeds, or Washington letters, or Audubon prints. Audubon once had his home on the Perkiomen, you know."

Well, I weakened, and that's the way I got started. We began going up and down the Perkiomen Valley, talking our way first into the kitchen, and if our luck held out, finally, into the attic. In a short time I was fortunate in picking up several old books with hand-tooled leather bindings, and pages as crisp as when they came from the press.

These two books mark the beginning of my Pennsylvania Dutch library. They are Schwenkfelder, religious in nature. The printing—not really printing as we think of it, but a printed script done by hand, a work of infinite patience and artistry—and the magnificent leather bindings, as American as cowboy boots, are the workmanship of Christopher Hoffman, a Schwenkfelder farmer, pastor, teacher, and bookbinder who once lived in Lower Salford Township, Montgomery County.

The beautiful script printing of these books is most outstanding. The Schwenkfelders, a small religious group from Silesia, in the eastern part of old Germany, were regarded as radicals by both the Roman Catholic Church and by the various Protestant groups, the Lutherans in particular. Their antagonists had considerable political prestige and succeeded in getting a law passed prohibiting the printing of all Schwenkfelder books and tracts. The penalties were very great and were to be inflicted upon both the authors and the publishers. Consequently there was no one who would risk his neck printing for the small and persecuted Schwenkfelder group. And what did they do about it? They began at once learning the book-binding art and training scribes in the manner of the illuminators of the Middle Ages. Soon they were producing their own books without the aid of printing presses and producing volumes of craftsmanship and artistry vastly superior to anything that has ever emerged from a printing press.

The two books which I possess have another interesting and significant feature. I refer to the telltale water marks—a three-leaved clover with the initials "W.R." This precious watermark calls attention to the old Rittenhouse Paper Mill on the Wissahickon, the first paper mill in the New World.

Pennsylvania pioneers built and operated the first paper mill in the Colonies. This mill was established about 1660 by William and Nicholas Rittenhouse. The Rittenhouse family, the older spelling being Rittinghuysen, lived at Müehlheim, Germany, where the making of fine paper was an established craft. Young William migrated to Holland and while there happened upon some of William Penn's tracts telling of the good life in Pennsylvania and inviting all those who desired to share in the Holy Experiment to come to the New World. William Rittenhouse was a pious Mennonite. He could not turn his back upon such an opportunity and soon determined to go to Pennsylvania, to the region of Germantown where he understood there were many Mennonites, and there he would build a paper mill and continue in his chosen work.

Upon his arrival at Philadelphia, William Rittenhouse was encouraged by William Bradford, an established printer, to build that paper mill. Apparently Bradford helped him get started but hardly to the extent suggested in a letter which Bradford penned to a friend saying, "Samuel Carpenter and I are Building a Paper-Mill about a Mile from thy Mills at Skulkill, and hope we shall have Paper within less than four months."

The first printed reference to the Rittenhouse Paper Mill appears in some lines of doggerel verse written by Pennsylvania's first poet, Richard Frame, and published in a book printed by William Bradford in 1692:

> A Paper Mill near German-Town doth stand,
> So that the Flax, which first springs from the
>   Land,
> First Flax, then Yarn, and then they must begin,
> To weave the same, which they took pains to
>   spin.
> Also, when on our backs it is well worn,
> Some of the same remains Ragged and Torn:
> Then of these Rags our Paper it is made,
> Which in process of time doth waste and fade:
> So what comes from the Earth, appeareth plain,
> The same in Time returns to Earth again.

The Pennsylvania Saints not only built the first paper mill; they also established their printing presses and had them in greater number than any other Colony. Not all the printing presses were set up by the Saints; there was, for example, Ben Franklin's, who despite his many virtues neither thought himself a saint nor would condone anyone adorning him with a halo. Franklin's press was, however, bilingual, turning out many German books as well as English. While the Dutch patronized Franklin, they had their own presses, too, and presses that equalled or surpassed those of their more illustrious competitor. There were the Christopher Saur press at Germantown, and the press at the Ephrata Cloisters which printed German almost exclusively.

Much routine printing was done on the Pennsylvania presses in response to the demands of a primitive agricultural and economic community; for example, the many almanacs. And there was the necessary printing of government notices, laws, ordinances, and money. But what did they do beyond these bread-and-butter things?

This was the question that was uppermost in my mind when Frederick and I began pounding doors, persuading alert "Hausfrauen," who often acquitted themselves as excellent watchdogs, that we really meant no harm, nor would we walk away with the kitchen sink. Often we had to talk as fast as lightning-rod peddlers, meanwhile edging our way toward the attic.

A Pennsylvania Dutch attic is a thrilling and never-to-be-forgotten sight. There was Emily Schall's attic, big as a barn—and that of Adelina Fuchs, a little difficult to get into, but rewarding beyond belief. Bags of schnitz, slabs of bacon, and home dry-cured hams hanging from the rafters; portraits and paintings of the ancestors looking down from the walls; onions, nuts, and seed corn in their allotted spaces on the floor; spinning wheels, a cobbler's bench, sleigh bells, old button shoes, ladies' dresses, hats, corsets and other unmentionables and, of course, no-tions, magazines, books—all jumbled together like the ingredients in a nightmare.

Frederick and I limited our attention pretty largely to the books and magazines as we went from attic to attic. We were not alone in our quest. There were many people looking for choice antiques—plank chairs, a stray piece of Gaudy Dutch, a Stiegel sugar bowl, an antique clock or rifle. Everyone knew that such Dutch stuff was valuable, and surely nothing could have been said against a vigilant "Hausfrau" had she defended them with a pitchfork in her hand.

But with us the situation was a little different. Again and again I was greeted with the words, "Du bisht der Parre, ain't?"

I was happy to answer truthfully and to add, "We're not interested in antiques. We're looking for old Bibles and old religious books."

Often, to our delight the response was, "Vell, don't stand ous dere in der colt. Cum in. Nobody vants olt buchs un papers—vy, it's chust junk, ain't?" With the guard down we moved in and took over.

Interesting and productive as the attics were, we discovered richer veins in which to dig. We did much digging, and that is the correct word, in a deserted chicken house. Over by Silverdale—a village as inviting as it sounds—in the much coveted Bucks County region, there is a chicken house with a huge nest full of old books. Levi Yoder, the beloved antique dealer, often brought home books by cartons, even truck loads, and into the chicken house he tossed them. There they languished helter-skelter until someone with a strong back and an equally strong will engaged in the digging and sorting. The tonnage was considerable, the pay dirt limited, and yet from time to time something emerged that was well worth the having.

It was in this chicken house that I came upon my first Saur Bible. I shall never recover from the thrill of that title page:

> *Biblia, Das ist: Die Heilige Schrift . . .*
> *Germantown: Gedruckt bey Christoph Saur,*
> *1743.*

That Bible served to refresh my mind. I began thinking about Christopher Saur (the name is spelled in various ways—Sauer, Sour, Sower, Saur) one of the Saints who never failed to give the Holy Experiment unconditional priority. He was rightly distressed that no Bibles, other than one for the Indians, had been printed in the New World, and he was determined to rectify this grievous neglect. When he opened his shop at Germantown, he hung upon the wall a motto, *"Zur Ehres Gottes un der Naechsten Bestes"*—To the glory of God and the neighbor's good. Moreover, he was determined in time to implement this motto with a plan of action.

Saur, who had mastered some thirty different trades, including those of carpenter, physician, tailor, wheelwright, glazier, typesetter, and clockmaker, set about focusing all his energies upon one goal—an American edition of God's Holy Word. To this end he imported type and paper from Europe. The ink he manufactured on his own—nutgall and chimney soot to make it black; gum arabic to give it body; and vinegar to make it thin.

The Saur objective envisioned a long and arduous task and few people believed that it could ever be brought to a successful conclusion. Despite the seemingly insuperable difficulties, difficulties that other printers pointed out in declining the venture, Saur printed the first page in April 1742. A year went by with every hand, every muscle, every energy bent upon the production of that American Bible. Spring gave way to another summer. Finally, one hot summer day Christopher Saur lifted the last page from the press. The first "American" Bible was a reality and all "To the glory of God and the Neighbor's good." Such was the Bible that I dug out of the chicken house at Silverdale.

I kept going back to that chicken house year after year. By and by I turned up the Saur 1763 Bible, the first to be printed on American paper; and the Saur 1776 Bible, the first to be printed with American type. Concerning this third Bible the legend persists that the British soldiers, quartered in Philadelphia while the American forces were at Valley Forge, used many of its unbound pages to bed down their horses during the cold winter nights. It could be true, but there is no evidence to support this claim. As a matter of fact the 1776 edition is the one that is easiest to come by.

After finding the Bible, there was the matter of putting the hard cash down on the line. Fortunately, Levi was not a difficult man to deal with. He seemed always to consider the energy I had expended in digging out the "find" as an adequate down payment. As to the rest, he operated on the same basis Saur did when he advertised his first Bible, "eighteen shillings, but to the poor and needy we have no price."

The Pennsylvania Saints knew that without the Bible neither they nor their Holy Experiment could long endure. Forty years after Saur's first Bible became as manna for the Dutch, the wants of the English-speaking pioneers were supplied by Robert Aitken, who, with the encouragement of the United States Congress, printed the first American Bible in the English tongue. I had the good fortune to find an Aitken Bible. Though doubtless the English Saints read it, the Dutch Saints preserved it. And what a place to find a rare English Bible: the top shelf of a Mennonite harness shop!

The Menno Weaver Harness Shop and Church Supply Depot stands out all by its lonesome in the Lancaster County tobacco fields near Blue Ball. It's strictly Dutch, friendly Mennonite, loosely business in its ways. With the Weavers harness comes first and then comes heaven. Nothing else matters. The smell of the newly cured leather, like the incense in a cathedral, permeates the entire institution. The walls and rafters are hung with horse collars, hames, sweat pads, bridles, and belly bands, all of them made by Weaver hands on the very spot. The tooling and sewing of the harness are not only good craftsmanship but show the inherent Pennsylvania Dutch artistry.

Once when I stopped at the Weaver harness shop a distinguished clergyman, M. Stephen James, from New York, accompanied me. He was much taken by the harness and was delighted when Menno consented to make him a belt. After a few hours we returned; the belt carefully tooled and sewed awaited us. Menno showed us the finished product with obvious pride, dimly aware, perhaps, that not many of his belly bands would be seen on Fifth Avenue. He began figuring out the price tag, "Sivitzich un Ninetzay fer der Schnell—(buckle) . . . dat vill give nein un ochtzich."

I explained, "It'll cost you eighty-nine cents."

But Menno remembered and interrupted, "Ach, ich fergess, du bisht ein Parre, ain't? Mit der discount—ayn un ochtzich."

Eighty-one cents for a belt one would be proud to wear down Fifth Avenue in the Easter parade, use through the years, and then pass on to the coming generations.

My Aitken Bible was a bargain, too. I was rummaging behind the harness on the upper shelf. A book fell and hit me on the head: a Bible. I glanced at it and decided it had little or no value, but inasmuch as it had been a disappointing day I kept the Bible and picked out several other old books that were far from exciting and a couple of antique bottles that struck my fancy, empty, to be sure. Menno looked over the lot; did some calculating and came up with the total: 'Füenf un tzwanzich," which, with the discount, meant I was twenty-three cents out of pocket.

On the way home I had a hunch. Did it fit the description of the Bible my neighbor Frederick was always looking for? I stopped the car and began examining it. There it was clear and bold on the title page:

The Holy Bible, Containing the Old and New Testaments: Newly translated out of the Original Tongues; And with the former Transla-

tions Diligently compared and revised. Phila-
delphia: Printed and Sold by R. Aitken, at
Pope's Head, Three doors above the Coffee
House, in Market Street. M.DCC, LXXXII.

The Aitken Bible, though authorized and in a sense
underwritten by the United States' Congress, is, unlike
the Saur Bibles, not an imposing volume that commands
instant respect, and to be truthful about it, neither the
paper nor the printing is first class. Its poor workmanship
doubtless accounts for its extreme rarity today. My copy,
however, is something special, with a unique appeal. The
leather binding bears the round gouge-marks of a bit.
Evidently some carpenter with brace-and-bit in his hands
used the old Book as a buffer to protect the cutting edge
of his precious tools. How true of the Bible—it has often
proved a buffer when the going is rough, and I have come
to appreciate the telltale gouge marks that adorn my copy.

When I first came across the Aitken Bible I little valued
it, and the price, twenty-three cents—forgetting about the
other books and the bottles—failed to stimulate a right
appreciation. Some years later I came to understand the
value a modern bibliophile sets upon an Aitken Bible,
when a Boston book dealer flew to Reading to purchase a
copy for $1600. Having flushed and bagged his game he
was so happy with his acquisition that he went out and
forthwith got himself drunk on Reading beer, so drunk
that he couldn't make the scheduled return but lay over,
sobered up, and flew back the next day.

It was in Menno Weaver's harness shop that I came
across another interesting book containing the first treatise on music written in the Western Hemisphere. Though

the book was printed in 1747 it had not travelled far during the years, for the Ephrata Cloister, the place of its authorship and printing, is but a short distance from the harness shop, and if you strike out across the corn and tobacco fields, you will find it a pleasant Sunday afternoon stroll. The Book, *Das Gesang Der Turtle Taube,—* The Song of the Turtle Dove—contains the hymns of the Seventh-Day Baptists and a preface entitled "The Art of Song."

The author, Johann Conrad Beissel, known also by his monastic name, Brother Friedsam, was in at least one respect like the other Pennsylvania Saints; he was a lover of music. He had come to the "wilderness" of the New World to offer up his life in prayer and communion with God. But even the prayer life called for praise, and it was easier to praise God in the company of the faithful than to do it in a corner all alone. The instinct to praise saved Beissel from becoming what he aspired to be: one of the "solitary."

The Cloister Buildings, some of them still standing and well worth a visit, were soon filled with praise: choirs singing seven-part music, and the Saints creating melodies and writing out hymns in delicate fraktur, ornamented in subdued color, with tulips, lilies, birds, angels, and the Virgin Sophia in an harmonious perfusion.

The Ephrata Saints differed in many ways from their equally Dutch neighbors. They tried to live the life of the Godly Solitary, keeping the Seventh Day holy, bending low to walk through doors better designed for dogs than humans, sleeping on their hard wooden shelves with little blocks of wood under their necks for pillows, observing the monastic hours so that there was more prayer than sleep, and subjecting themselves to outlandish dietary restrictions. The members of the Order wore the Capuchin garb, the women being vested in white for solemn occasions. Assembled in the Saal, robed in long white vestments, bathed beneath the flickering light of the candles, they must have looked, even as they sounded, like an angel choir.

In his treatise on music Father Friedsam lays extraordinary emphasis upon dietary restrictions and advises, as I translate from the preface of my *Turtle Taube:*

> Care must be taken of the body and its requirements reduced to a minimum, so that the voice may be angelic, heavenly, pure and clear . . . All meat dishes quite discommode us . . . milk causes heaviness, butter makes indolent and dull; honey provides brightness to the eyes but not a clear voice. Of the common vegetables potatoes and beets are best. Beans are too heavy, satiate too much and tend to arouse impure desires. Of drink, nothing is better than pure clear water, or water to which a little bread has been added to make a soup.

The Ephrata Saints excelled in song and in fraktur. They were also successful with their printing press, producing the largest book printed in the Colonies, the much prized, *Der Blutige Schau-Platz Oder Martyrer Spiegel . . . Ephrata MDCCXLVIII.* This book, commonly called the "Martyr's Mirror," was job work done for the Mennonites after other printers had asserted the task was beyond the possibility of execution in the New World. But doing the impossible was the business of the Ephrata Saints.

First of all there was the translation. To this labor Peter Miller, known also as Prior Jabez, was assigned. The Dutch text of Holland had to be converted into the German text of the Pennsylvania Dutch, and that for an extra-size volume of over fifteen hundred pages. To accomplish this task Peter Miller toiled twenty hours daily for three years—a sweatshop operation if ever there was one. This same Peter Miller is reputed to be the man who, at the urging of George Washington, consented to translate the Declaration of Independence into the various European languages, a work which he did unaided and alone, refusing any remuneration whatsoever.

The "Martyr's Mirror" is remarkable in other ways. With the most primitive of tools and a few pieces of crude machinery they produced a quality of paper that after two centuries causes experts to stand in awe. The type likewise obliges one to marvel. As I page the book I can find scarcely a single blurred or faded letter, and I am told that the four hundred gallons of ink which they used were made of such ingredients as flaxseed oil, chimney soot, oak galls and the juice of pokeberries. Where there is devotion there is a way. I almost forgot, my copy was found in a Dutch attic, as you might guess.

The Solitary of Ephrata were also fertile in theological speculation. While they kept themselves unspotted from the world, they were not the kind to hide their light under a bushel. They wrote Benjamin Franklin of their theological beliefs, kept His Holiness, the Pope, on their mailing list, and ventured to attract the attention of the British Royal Family. There is a tradition that the English Court sent a special commission to Ephrata in order to hear their singing. In time, as the story goes, a gift box from the Royal family came to Brother Friedsam. But Brother Friedsam was concerned about the favor of God; he didn't give a hoot for the favor of kings, so without opening the box he promptly buried it.

The Pennsylvania Saints have pioneered in diversified ways. Far from being the "dumb Dutch" as they are sometimes referred to, their cultural achievements are noteworthy and enduring, and in so many instances they have been first. There was Daniel Pastorius who in 1688 brought forth the first scientific treatise. Incidentally, he wrote fluently in eight languages, no mean accomplishment for a Saint who lived in a cave. There was Christopher Saur with his American edition of the Bible, seven editions of the New Testament, and the first religious magazine. There was the *Schul Ordnung*, the first American treatise on pedagogy written by Christopher Dock in 1754 and published by Christopher Saur in 1770. There were the Ephrata publications: Van Braght's *Martyrer Spiegel*, the largest book printed in the Colonies, and the *Turtle Taube* containing the first American essay on music. There was the Rittenhouse Paper Mill, and let us not forget David Rittenhouse who in 1769 made the first approximately accurate calculation of the distance of the earth from the sun. Of him, Thomas Jefferson said, "He has not, indeed, made a world, but he has approached nearer to its Maker than any man who has lived from the creation to this day."

As I contemplate the achievements of these Pennsylvania Saints my thoughts go back to my friend Dan and his farm in the Dutch country. I can understand why he came back to the place where he was born and why he insists, "The birds sing best in Pennsylvania."

4—"Hex Vill Make Ous"

"TELL ME, Annie, what do you know about Hex?"
Annie's fan moved faster. Her busy tongue became strangely silent; her countenance fell. There was no answer—only the melancholy intrusion of a summer evening's invisible eavesdropper, "Whippoorwill, whippoorwill, whippoorwill." It was too dark for adequate vision and that forced Annie to weigh my tone carefully to determine whether I was merely trotting out a new conversational theme for lighthearted chitchat, or whether perhaps in a censorius mood I was setting a trap for her, or whether with urgent sincerity I was asking because I had in mind an ill friend or perhaps even some unmentioned affliction of my own.

There is more to the Pennsylvania Dutch than backdoor English and shoofly pie. Just as the soil of the Dutch Country is rich and deep, so also there is a mysterious depth to the Dutch Saints that only years of intimate fellowship can begin to reveal. First you must ease your way into their homes and into their hearts. Later, perhaps, they will come your way, sit down at your table, and "make down der bet fer der night." Then you will discover that they are like the soil they till: rich, deep, and good. But scratch a Dutchman a little too deep and you will also discover stratum of the primitive in him. The same is true of all men. Basically, as the modern pyschiatrist insists upon reminding us, we are all primitive, each in his own way. "Hex vill make ous."

Annie had come to our house with her husband as chauffeur and silent companion. It was a hot evening with just a little breeze oozing across the front porch. The sun was banked down for the night, the heavens salted with stars, and the whippoorwill, night prowler that he is, had just come to life. He seemed bent upon monopolizing the audio part of the picture. His harsh, haunting cry—partly avian, partly human, partly supernatural—was not in vain.

That question, "What do you know about Hex?" caused Annie to ponder. Since she wasn't sure, she picked her steps with care. "Well, now," she ventured, "don't tell me that you never heard of old man Leffler—he lived there at the bottom of Kugler's Hill. He could blow for burns, and stop blood when no doctor could. That whole Leffler bunch had something when it came to healing. Everybody went to them in the old days; at least that's the story they tell me."

She paused to feel her way. I led her on.

"Yes, Annie, I knew the Lefflers—the next generation— they still had the reputation. Plenty of people were afraid of them, but there was always someone going in or out and nearly everyone agreed they were either bootleggers or powwowers."

"Don't you believe it—I mean that bootleg business. They had dandelion wine; I helped them make it more than once. And wild cherry, too, the best you ever drank; and a little "Schnaps," no doubt, in the medicine chest, but they weren't the drinking kind. And money, heavens, no; they had plenty. Those people came to the Lefflers for help. Many a baby was snapped out of a colic fit, just like that—"

"But, Annie," I interrupted, "I've heard about the Lefflers. What I'm after is what you know. You can powwow, can't you?"

More silence—then slowly the gate swung open.

she was doing all her work and I lost my first job.

"Scott, there's power, terrible power, for better or for worse, in those three highest names. Tomorrow I'll teach you how to do it. I'm tired now, and we better all go to bed."

I went to bed but not to sleep. All manner of Hex lore kept bubbling in my head. Again and again my thoughts went back to the stone hills of Montgomery County and to Grandmother Schwartz who wearied through her last days in an old tumbled-down house near where the Medinger pottery stood. She was extremely poor—poor in money, food, clothing, shelter, friends, health. All that she had were memories, long memories in a lonely lane where the shadows of fear and superstition had free play. She had virtually no callers except "der Parre," her pastor, to whom she laid bare the secrets that haunted her soul. I recalled how she always talked of the "good old days" and sooner or later got round to a whispered conversation about old Kate Kirker who was known as the "Hex Kate."

As I remember her telling it, Grandmother Schwartz was only a little girl in the days when Old Kate filled the stone hills with mystery and fear. But Grandmother remembered Old Kate all too well, remembered and described the red mark on Kate's face, remembered the funeral, too, and how they tried to hide that red mark but without success. Old Kate had moldered in her grave for more than fifty years, but when Grandmother Schwartz told about her it was always in a whisper so that I got the feeling that "die Hex Kate" was outside the door listening at the keyhole.

That Old Kate was a Hex was firmly established, at least in the mind of Grandmother Schwartz. The evidence was substantial, and, as I recall, hinged primarily upon two incidents, the first involving a little girl named Mary, the second involving Grandmother Schwartz's people. As I tossed on my pillow that night the whole thing came back to me and I heard it again in Grandmother's words, just as she had so often told it.

"Ach vell, dere vas strange doings in dem days. Little Mary vas about three or four ven everybody seen dat she was failing so. She vouldn't eat; she got sinner un sinner. Every day she asked fer crackers un milk un took dem ous mit her fer to play. But still she got sinner yet. Vone day her Papa spied on her. Un vat did he see? Mary put her milk un crackers in a saucer un uff cumpt a big, fat blacksnake un began to eat, vile Mary stroked un petted un talked mit it like it vas a baby doll. Papa rushed uff mit a big club un killed der snake."

"Now, Grandmother," I intruded. "I don't like snake stories. Guess I better be going."

"Ach, no, Parre, You can't go yet. Vy dis iss no snake story. Chust you listen to vat comes now vonct. Little Mary vouldn't eat. She chust cried un cried. The doctor couldn't help. Den dey knew she vas hexed. Un vat did dey do? Dey vent ous un dug uff dat big blacksnake, put it on a pile of strawy manure un set it on fire. Before der fire vas ous, who came running but Old Kate. Her stove had exploded, burnt her hands un arms. She vanted baking soda un butter. Dey knew besser, un told her dey didn't have none. Old Kate turned avay wringing her hands in pain. She never bossered dem no more. Mary began to eat un soon vas fat as all get-out."

I remembered being obliged to agree with her that it was an interesting story and was on the point of asking a question or two, but Grandmother Schwartz had no time for questions or answers, for she was determined to tell me "chust one more story before you go."

"Now I must tell you about der ret mark that vas on Old Kate's face."

"Yes, Grandmother," I interrupted, "what kind of a red mark was that?"

"Vell, now, chust you vait. It was ret like a birthmark iss, un people sought dat's vat it vas, but dat it vasn't. I know, for mine Vater un Mutter told me all about it. Old Kate never had a ret mark before she hexed Mama's cream."

Grandmother Schwartz thought she heard someone at the door. She went, investigated carefully, and as she came back to her chair commented, "Ach, it vas nossings. Chust der vind, maybe." She resumed her story, this time in a strictly whispered conversation, insisting upon having her mouth close to my ear.

"Vell, it vas dis vay. Now you know vat a churn iss like mit der handle dat you stomp uff un down?"

I assured her that I knew and encouraged her by adding that I had operated such a churn as a boy.

"Vone day Mama churned un churned un der butter chust wouldn't make. Papa came in fer supper but Mama vas still churning. She had done everysing, added haesse vasser, added old butter but still it vouldn't make. Papa sought long un finally sait, 'My Gott, you don't sink it's forhexed, do you?' Vell, my Pop vent un got a horseshoe. Un vat did he do? He put it in der stove un made it ret hot. Den he plunged it into der churn. It vonders me how, but right avay der butter cum. 'Now look,' said Pop, 've vill see who has der ret mark.' Dat very night Kate Kirker cum to der door. Ven der light fell on her face, der vas der ret mark chust like a horseshoe."

As I finally tumbled off to sleep I could hear Grandmother observing, "Old Kate took dat mark to her grave. Dey tried to make it cuvered fer der funeral but dey couldn't cuver it uff. Kate lived a Hex, she vas buried a Hex—in life un in death der Hex mark showed strough . . ."

The next morning, after breakfast, Annie kept her promise and initiated me into the secrets of what the Pennsylvania Dutch call "Sympathetic Medicine" but what the outside world refers to as Hex, or powwow, or black magic, or witchcraft. With many a story Annie encouraged me as I wrote down the instructions. She told me of this cure and of that, naming people and places, and usually adorning her simple tales with a wealth of local color.

I asked her about the bleeding bone-handles on the knives and forks at the old Hosensack Inn and the murder story connected with it. She insisted she had never heard the story, so I was obliged to tell her. It happened just before the Civil War. A stranger came to the Inn. He was a handsome fellow with a tongue equally smooth in English and in Dutch. He tried to pass himself off as a Dutch Saint, but in this his success was rather limited. Most of the time he spent in the bar room. He was a good customer whose chief delight was in boasting that he could hold more liquor than any other man. With women he also had a way, though most of the local Dutch girls remained aloof. Several city "darlings" kept visiting him from time to time. Money—there was no bottom to his pocket. He didn't hesitate to buy friends, or at least to try.

Suddenly he dropped out of sight. A week later the buzzards kept circling over the hill behind the Inn. Down in the ravine they found his body. He was gagged; his hands and feet were tied with bailing wire. A deep cross was gouged into each wrist—he had bled to death.

The police were called in. The clues were few. Such clues as they did turn up proved sterile. As a last resort they sent into the Blue Mountain and brought down an old woman wise in the ways of Hex craft. She advised them to dig up the body which they had buried a few days previous, saw out several of the ribs and shape them into handles for knives and forks. This they did. The cutlery was given to the Inn. One day a nervous woman with shifting eyes, elegantly dressed, and inviting in her manners sat down at the table and took the cutlery into her hands. Instantly the blood began dripping from those bone handles.

Annie laughed at the tale. "Might be," she conceded, "but I never heard of it—I'd say it's just a tall story and you're the sucker."

I felt obliged to refresh my memory and contribute something substantial to the cause. I told her of my Grandmother who had erysipelas many years ago and how in a few hours almost half of her body was as though it were on fire. One of the older boys set off on horse-back to summon a physician from the village. Mean-while, an old German neighbor by the name of Uhlman came by. He said to Grandmother:

"Lizzie, you must be in terrible pain with that wild-fire."

"That I am," she answered, "Oh, I wish the doctor would come."

"I can heal you, Lizzie, if you want me to."

Instantly she pleaded, "If there's anything you can do, do it."

He stroked her face three times and mumbled some-thing. Then with his thumb he began at her forehead and marked off half her body, meanwhile saying, "When did this burning begin?"

"At breakfast time I noticed it."

"So long as it was coming, so long it will be in going away," he said.

Later that day the doctor came. They told him that Uhlman had been there. He didn't bother opening his bag but contented himself with the confession, "Uhlman can do more for erysipelas than I can."

I told her, also, of one of the most learned men I have ever known, an old Schwenksville neighbor, down along the Perkiomen, who was by any standard a scholar, and a man of scientific bent. Frederick Hillbiber had made a name for himself in the scientific world on account of his achievements in the field of mineralogy; he was a master of languages; his home was filled with historical and scientific books; his head was crammed with diversi-fied lore. We were intimate friends, for I was rightly concerned with the crumbs that fell from this wise man's table. One day I told him of a friend that had undergone major surgery in a hospital and who had almost bled to death upon the operating table. "Why didn't you tell me?" he asked. "I can stop bleeding."

"But this happened twelve miles away," I said.

Then he looked me straight in the eye, and slowly answered, "That would make no difference."

My doubts I kept from Annie as best I could. Nor did we discuss how powwow is losing its attraction for the younger generations of Pennsylvania Dutch. That it enjoyed a wide vogue in the days of the pioneer is easy to understand. In every crisis there is always some person who cries, "Do something," and someone is sure to respond. Others will nod approval, counselling, "It won't do any harm, anyway." Thus the virgin hills and valleys of Penn's "Sylvania" with its extensive pioneer population and its scarcity of physicians was a natural for the cultivation of folk healing arts.

Moreover, it might be pointed out that in the early days of the Commonwealth there was little to commend the "Practitioner in physic," as the medical doctor was then termed, over the "practitioner in sympathetic medicine." Indeed, it might be argued that the possibility of recovery was greater under the ministration of the Hex doctor. In those days the medical man's chief stock in trade was bloodletting. If no improvement materialized, he could resort to "golden heart powder," or "besoar powders" which were pulverized gall stones taken from animals native of Peru and the East Indies. If this didn't work, and your guess is as good as mine, there was always the possibility of more cutting and cupping for blood, with, in the end, positive relief assured—death.

The practice of folk healing through "sympathetic medicine" or Hexerei was an import which was brought here by our rugged pioneers. It had no difficulty in obtaining an indigenous status, and in time there were those who not only practiced it but promoted it, for the American genius is not slow in discerning something that can be made to pay off. One of these promoters was an illusive Dutchman named John George Hohman. In the year 1819 he published a book at Reading, Pennsylvania, entitled *Der Lange Verborgene Freund*—The Long Lost Friend. This book went through many editions and was published in half a dozen places or more, a kind of "Bible" for all who practiced powwow. A copy of Hohman's *Long Lost Friend* was given to me by a dear old woman who, having lived by it, treasured it and had it fitted into a protective tin case. She assured me that it had gone unscathed through a flood and a fire, a sure proof of its divine approval. She told me that she had prayed about it and I was the man who was to have it, and she added, "It might safe your life, or vone of your dear ones, ain't?"

It is easy to understand how such a conviction would lay hold upon her. On the very first and last pages of the Hohman book, set in heavy type and surrounded by three crosses, are these words:

> Whoever carries this book with him, is safe from all his enemies, visible or invisible; and whoever has this book with him, cannot die without the holy corpse of Jesus Christ, nor

be drowned in any water, nor burn up in any
fire, nor can any unjust sentence be passed
upon him.

A reading of the book scarcely supports the above
assurance, for it betrays certain psychological techniques,
a pinch of common sense here and there, and a vast
quantity of superstition, some in crudest form. And,
believe me, I am describing it as sympathetically as I
know how. Its chief merit is that everyone is interested
in a cure-all and it offers many prescriptions of this nature. Here is one that Hohman prescribed:

Whoever carries the right eye of a wolf fas-
tened inside his right sleeve, remains free from
all injuries.

The cure of warts is an old story and one that I've
seen work in my own family. The orthodox way, for the
powwower, is, of course, the use of words, and then an
apple or an onion is rubbed over the warts and buried
under a rainspout. The way of the book is somewhat
different, it reads:

Roast chicken feet and rub the warts with them,
then bury them under the eaves.

Before the days of Pasteur there was need of a treatment for those bitten by rabid animals, especially dogs.
Hohman offers what he terms a "security against mad
dogs" which may have been very efficacious, especially
if the dog were not really mad. Based upon the old adage
that "prevention is the best cure," it laid emphasis upon
an early application. One was to address the animal
saying:

Dog hold thy nose to the ground, God has made me and thee, hound! (Then comes the all-important rubric.) This you must repeat in the direction of the dog; and the three crosses you must make toward the dog, and the words must be spoken before he sees you.

As a boy I remember being told that the practice of the veterinarian differed chiefly from that of the physician in the greater strength of the medicine. This, it would appear, is confirmed by the Hohman book. There is a certain restraint in the treatment of humans, but God pity the poor cows and those who doctor them! Here is his "method of treating a sick cow":

The cross of Jesus Christ poured out milk; J.
The cross of Jesus Christ poured out water; J.
The cross of Jesus Christ has poured them out.

These lines must be written on three pieces of white paper, then take the milk of the sick cow and these three pieces of paper, put them in a pot, and scrape a little of the skull of a criminal; close it well, and put over a hot fire, and the witch will have to die. If you take the three pieces of paper, with the writing on them, in your mouth, and go out before your house, speak three times, and then give them to your cattle, you shall not only see all the witches, but your cattle will also get well again.

One doesn't need to page far into the Hohman book until there is an almost irresistible temptation to lower the boom and be done with this messy caldron of witch's brew. The temptation should be at least tempered with the realization that the practice of powwow is of necessity conceived in secrecy and maintained in mystery. It is not for the curious or the profane. It is not for sale. The inmost secrets of this ancient practice will never be exposed to the public gaze, for neither conniving, nor bribery, nor torture can avail that end. Hohman knew, as I well know, that we are here confronted by mysterious realities that cannot be unveiled in print. Consequently Hohman, in his book, was obliged to content himself with the chaff that blows over the fence. A true understanding of the powwow technique can be acquired only through oral tradition. A male, if he wishes, may pass on the secrets to a female; a woman may convey the mystery to a man. Annie could whisper it in my ear, and she did. Much as I might like to broadcast it to my friends, I am not at liberty to do so. Let me add that even to one who does not believe in Hexerei, there are some confidences too sacred to be put in books.

Reading about this Hex business in an old powwow book reveals an incredibly insipid and stupid concoction; but when you learn of it by ear, listening to one who has practiced it or benefited by it, especially if it be the sincere, persuasive voice of one like Annie accompanied with the plaintive overtones of an illusive whippoorwill, the thing is unbelievably and gloriously transfigured, taking on terrestrial import and celestial significance. Long after the practice of Hexerei has ceased, if that time ever comes, the splendor of its achievements will live on in fancy and story—an unforgettable part of the Pennsylvania Dutch saga.

Time was when a Dutchman, widely known as a leader and orator, lifted his voice in the halls of government. When he spoke, multitudes listened. This silver-tongued orator was once a shy Dutch boy with an impediment in his speech. It was so bad that the teacher couldn't understand him, and the school kids made fun of him. Old Aunt Lizzie could take it no longer. She had the boy stand against a peach tree in the back yard. She put a level on the top of his head and marked the tree; then she drilled a hole at the place of the mark. By and by she got three hairs from the boy's head. One moonlight night when the sign was right she poked the hairs into the hole and plugged it with secret words and the good earth of the Dutch country. It worked out just as she hoped and predicted—as the boy outgrew the mark so he also outgrew his affliction. Believe it or not, it takes but three little hairs to loose a Dutchman's tongue.

The hair of a Dutchman may look like that of any other human but there is a difference. Red head, black head, or one that's nearly bald—if it happens to be the head of a Dutch saint, that hair is of tremendous significance. Three little hairs may assure good luck: a quick marriage, a baby boy, an inheritance from an unknown cousin, a recovery from tuberculosis or cancer, yes, even an escape from a hangman's noose. Three little hairs may compel ill fortune: a jilted love, a miscarriage, a barn or house on fire, a baby with club feet, a stroke, and even insanity.

There was power in the hair of Samson, but when Delilah cut that hair Samson became weak as a cat. There is power in the hair of every Dutchman—power for good, power for evil. If you come by three hairs from the head of an enemy, all you need is a hole in the wall or a hole in a tree and the all-powerful words of Hexerei and that enemy will be as a worm under the heel of your shoe. You can drive him crazy, bring him to death by inches, or put him out of the way with a stroke. Because in the Dutch country so much can hang upon a hair, there are many who, after combing or brushing their heads, carefully gather each loose hair and either burn them or bury them deep in the earth.

Three little hairs in your hand and you have a power that neither Napoleon nor Caesar knew. Three hairs of your sweetheart and you can force her against her will, three hairs and no fire can hurt you, no illness can afflict you, no thief molest you, no evil eye fall upon you. Three little hairs and destiny is in your hands.

Those who visit the Pennsylvania Dutch country for the first time are sure to grab their cameras and try for a shot of the Amish. The Amish are an irresistible lure to the photographer but also a disappointing one. The adults, looking like Saints lifted from the Old Testament, and the children, like mischievous angels dressed for an outing in Mom's apron and Pop's pants, are enough to excite even a globetrotter.

Getting the picture—that's another story. Did you ever try catching grasshoppers? Well, they're easy compared with the Amish. Point a camera at them and they dodge, weave, turn, kick up their heels and run like colts in a pasture. If there is no way of escape, they stick out their tongues, make hideous faces, and if you get too close they may even spit in your face.

The Amish base their opposition to pictures upon the Commandment which forbids "any graven image." This, however, does not seem to explain fully their dread of the camera. We may safely conclude that superstition lurks somewhere in the picture. It may be that the concepts of certain primitive peoples are involved in this Amish taboo. There is, for example, among certain primitive tribes a fear that the soul, in part at least, passes from the person to the person's image or picture.

That something of this nature prompts the Amish to avoid all photography is suggested by an incident involving an Amish school girl. She reluctantly consented to have her picture taken with her class at school and after a time she smuggled the picture home. Her mother found it and turned over both the picture and the girl to her father for appropriate action. The father was violent in his wrath and began expressing himself, "I'll learn you. I never sought my daughter vould break der Law of Gott un bring down upon us his wrath. I have mind to club you gudt un lock you in der attic."

He began looking at the picture—the first picture he had ever seen of any member of his family. Red with rage and trembling, he was none the less speechless. Finally the girl had courage to open her mouth. "Papa, I'm sorry," she sobbed. "It iss a sin. Take it quick un burn it uff in der stove."

There was silence while Pop looked further at the little picture and slowly stroked his beard. Finally he said, "Nein, nein, dat I can't do. It looks too much like you. Here iss der picture. Do mit it vat you vill."

Moreover, in all candor, it must be conceded that the

superstition of our Dutch country is by no means limited to Hex. Somehow these wholesome, hardy people have tended to confuse the supernatural and the superstitious. For them the Bible, the signs of the Zodiac, the sign of the cross, the mystic tulip, prayer, magic, witchcraft, faith, and piety have tended to blur and to become one confused, mysterious pattern of life. True, the Word of God is for the Pennsylvania Dutchman the final source of authority, but he finds that "word" in many places. It's in the Bible by the bed, in the doctor book on the parlor table, in a copy of Hohman that may be hidden away in a closet, and surely in John Baer's *Agricultural Almanac* hanging between the kitchen range and the kitchen table and contesting this sanctum sanctorum with the choice ears of corn hanging there, seed for the coming year.

It is this precious almanac that tells him when to plant his crops, when to harvest them, when to cut weeds so that they'll die, how to dehorn the bull, when to prune the fruit trees, how to tell the weather. It's a thoroughly ecumenical volume designed to broaden one's interest and sharpen one's concern. It tells about the character of the constellations, planets and aspects, the lunar cycle, ember days, the chronology of the Jews, the chronology of the Mohammedans, the cardinal points, how to make funnel cakes and egg custards. No one can deny there's a liberal education in John Baer's Almanac.

What the almanac doesn't tell can be found in the heads of the Pennsylvania Dutch. Annie, for one, is saturated with this lore. The other night on the porch we were arguing about the best time to plant onions. Annie insisted that the moon must point down or the onions would come to the top of the ground and there would be no long tender shoots to munch upon. I brought her up short quoting my dad:

"Ich blans in der Grund, net der Mond,"—I plant in the ground, not in the moon.

Annie had heard that one before. She reached out her fingers. Running them through my thinning hair she said:

"Gott in Himmel, Scott—strubbly Kopf—you better look out or next thing you'll be as bald as a baby's behind. You don't have enough sense to know when to get your hair cut. Go get me the Almanac. I'll mark the dates."

Soon she was pouring over "Baer," marking all the days when the moon was on the increase and the sign was Leo. She kept saying, half to herself and half to me, "If you want a thick curly mane like a lion, it's got to be Leo."

While the Pennsylvania Dutch people are sometimes tempted to confuse the supernatural and the superstitious, they are nonetheless a people of deep religious faith. The Dutchman puts his hand into the hand of God and opens his heart to his fellow men. If, sometimes, by virtue of his faith, he seems to be led astray, his life is none the less richer and deeper because of it. There's more to him than backdoor English, and shoofly pie, and Hex that will, as he says, "make ous." He has everything that it takes to make a man—a brave, honest man who loves his neighbors and serves his God.

5—The Kingdom
Of The Tulip

THE Irish have their shamrock, the Scotch their heather, the Pennsylvania Dutch, the tulip; not the tulip of the springtime that roots in the earth and lifts its chalice heavenward, but the tulip of their folk art emblazoned on their barns as barn signs; painted on old dower chests; depicted on their tole or tin wear; glazed upon their pottery; and fraktured upon birth certificates, marriage documents, house blessings and bookplates; such is the tulip of the Saints.

The distinctive genius of the Pennsylvania Saints is nowhere so evident as in their folk art. This is now so widely known that the advertising world is beginning to cash in on it. As we drove through New England last summer we glimpsed in a cosy nook at the turn of the road a familiar flower, one I had believed was confined to Pennsylvania. There it was, an Ephrata lily—or we may call it a tulip—with gaudiest color, reaching from the ground to the top of the spacious barn door that was in reality no longer a barn door, but a tempting entrance to an antique shop.

Do not misunderstand me, the lily was not actually growing in the barren New England soil; it was a transplant—just so much advertising bait put on with brush and paint. But it worked. We braked, stopped, backed, turned and wormed our way round to the place where the flower was blooming, and entering, ruminated over a vast assembly of antiques and junk, mostly junk. As we examined item after item we were assured by one who talked in the proper Bostonian manner that each and every item was genuine—imported directly from Bucks, Montgomery, Lancaster, York, or Berks Counties.

The urge to buy Pennsylvania Dutch is inescapable. As I write, the Sunday *New York Times* and the *Pittsburgh Press* sprawl on the floor before the hearth. Looking up at me are the characteristic Dutch designs advertising bacon and ham, bologna and apple butter, noodles and pie fillings, Bucks County china and Lancaster County furniture. It is obvious that the folk art of the Saints is now worth its weight in hard cash.

The folk art of the Dutch is beautiful when looked upon from the outside; when seen from the inside it is something of infinite value. It is a kind of sacrament with an outer form and an inward grace. Unfortunately, however, it belongs largely to the past. There are few who practice it today and those who do are, for the most part, imitators who are content to copy rather than create.

One of the last of the folk artists among the Pennsylvania Saints was Irvin P. Mensch of Mensch Mill, not far from the Oley Valley down in Berks County. The old stone mill that ground the wheat to make the bread for Washington and his soldiers at Valley Forge is still standing; the last miller has long since departed. Likewise the Mensch home is there, but Irvin, the artist, is gone. Nevertheless, I shall always remember Mensch Mill and its babbling brook as it was when Irvin pursued his avocation: the art of illumination.

Irvin was a Pennsylvania Dutchman, fat and jovial, with a copious mane of white hair and a body of impressive muscles, the legacy of years of hard work. Nor was it difficult for him to maintain that muscle tone, for each day he continued to work at the creamery, churning butter, loading and unloading heavy crates, toting huge cans of milk here and there. Art was for him, as for all folk artists, strictly secondary. Every Dutchman knows that work comes before play. It was doubtless fortunate that this was his way, for a man with only one good eye must take care to relieve it by varying the nature of his work.

A New York clergyman friend (we men of the cloth often have no place to go except to visit one another) had stopped off for a few days. He became very much interested in the fraktur on my study walls and plied me with endless questions. I decided the best answer was to visit Irv Mensch, so down to Mensch Mill we went on a Sunday afternoon, knowing that day would make fewer demands upon our host.

"Well, well, Scott, come right in. Funny thing, I was just thinking about you yesterday—it's been a long time, you know."

"Thanks, Irv. How are you anyhow? Meet my friend Howard Hageman. He's from New York, but deep down there's a mess of Dutch in him—middle name Garberich, I believe."

Irv received Howard in the best of Dutch hospitality and presently began making excuses for the appearance of the house and of the artist as well.

"What a mess you caught me in, boys. The house is so 'dreckich,' as we say, and I'm so 'schtruwelich.' Why look at my shirt; it's all smeared with egg yellow. Oh, well, we'll forget it; guess you didn't come to see my shirt."

I explained to Irvin that I had told Howard about his

illuminated work, and expressed the wish that he would show us some of the illuminated envelopes he had sent his G. I. son in Japan. Those envelopes had slowed down the mails—every mailman taking them home to show his family and friends before he sent them on their way.

So far it was a matter of priming the pump. Then Howard began to take hold: "They tell me you have revived the medieval art of illumination."

"Well, hardly, my friend. I'm working at it—that I confess. Haven't mastered the technique by a long shot, but I'm making progress."

"Good! What about that manuscript volume you did for the Schwenkfelder Library at Pennsburg? They tell me it's a second Kells."

"Howard, I hate to tell you this; you can't believe everything our friend says. He's a little 'Blabbermaul' and too enthusiastic about my hobby. But wait, I've got a few early draft pages somewhere—if I can put my hands on them, they'll give you an idea."

Irv dug through a pile of papers and brought out a few of the pages with their gold Gothic letters, illuminated birds and flowers. Howard took them in his hands. "Right smack out of the Middle Ages; positively, they are."

"Well, boys, I feel that I know something about the medieval art, but lately I've gotten interested in this Dutch stuff. It's more exciting—but what a mess. That's why my shirt is such a sight. See that old Mensch Taufschein; you would call it a baptismal certificate. Look at that yellow capital "M" in the "Mensch," and the red on those tulips. There's egg in that yellow—I've proved that. Now

I'm working on the red—wouldn't mind kissing a girl with lips that color. Haven't got that red. More egg white or maybe more of the cherry-tree gum—you know the gum that oozes out of cherry trees?"

Howard was skeptical, "You mean to tell me that's the way they concocted that Dutch stuff?"

"Absolutely. I'm sure of it—nothing but a survival of the medieval art at the folk level. These pioneers did the best they could with what they had. No parchment, they used paper; no inks or colors, they made their own, just as I'm now trying to do. And look at these quills. Yanked them out of the Christmas goose—that's what they did in the old days."

We talked on and on and the subject was Pennsylvania Dutch fraktur, exclusively. As we were about to start home Irv took us over to the creamery and loaded us down with butter: "Here's a couple pounds apiece." Then as a parting word he slipped into the dialect, "Now, ven it's all, chust you-uns cum back un ve'll talk more fraktur, ain't?"

Well, Howard and I talked fraktur all the way home. I explained how many of the Plain People by reason of their religious restraints could not have pictures in their homes and how this was especially true of such groups as the Amish. With fraktur it was different. Even a school boy could dabble in it as he formed his ABCs, the most pious of Mennonite maids could practice it as she designed a colorful "Haus Segen" to hang on the wall, or a gay bookplate to put in the front of her *Unparthenisches Gesang-Buch.* The tulips, birds, and letters could be arranged with all the genius that imagination and artistry could command, and no Saint—lay or clerical—could take offense at that which so deftly blended art and faith in a reciprocal harmony.

Howard continued evidencing his interest with many questions. Finally he said, "Tell me how you got started in this business."

I no longer remember exactly how I told that story to Howard. It all happened one winter night—stormy as all-get-out. I had put on my slippers and settled down by the open fire with a book in my hands. The telephone rang. Into my ears came the sobs of a woman.

"Cum quick, Parre," she pleaded. She cleared her voice and continued, "Pop's eyes iss closed un he might any-time go, ain't?"

Snow, sleet, rain pelted down in baffling confusion, icing the roads, coating the windshield—that road was twisty, hilly, narrow as the devil. It was a terrible five miles that seemed to have no end. Was I glad when the bright lights of a Dutch kitchen fingered through the darkness to bid me welcome!

I shall never forget that winter night and the mad trip to see Pop, whose "eyes iss closed." They rushed me upstairs where I found everything just about as the girl had said. Pop lay in his Victorian bed with a headboard boasting intricate carvings and reaching toward the ceiling like the reredos behind a Church altar. His eyes were closed, his breathing heavy and irregular. It looked as though the end were imminent—after all, when one has passed ninety it ought not to be too hard to let go of life's plow—at least so it seems to those who are in their tenderfoot years.

The girls were on the mature side, approaching their seventies, and had doubtless speculated more than once as to which generation would go first. They were not only reconciled to the impending situation but I believe welcomed it as a working out of life's normal pattern. As Katie put it, "It's best dis vay. Vy who vould look after him if ve vas first to go, ain't?"

They had called me with a kind of Protestant last rites in mind. After all, we come into this world with that first ceremonial—a slap or two on the buttocks, we cry, and life begins. Should there not be last rites, a kind of God-speed for the long journey?

I had gotten off on the wrong foot that night. In my haste and in my anxiety about the weather, I had forgotten my pastoral service book, and I knew full well that they would prefer something from the book rather than something off the cuff. At such a time faith is best expressed through the accents of the ages. Not having my book, I said to Bessie, "I would like a Bible, please."

Bessie answered, "I 'low ve haf vone someveres."

After rather extended searching she came with a tremendous leather-bound tome: "It says B-i-b-l-i-a"—she spelled it out—"it makes like a Bible, ain't?"

I reassured her. Soon I was reading the Scripture, leading in prayer and in a commendation of the dying: "Lord, now lettest thou thy servant depart in peace." As I was about to return the Bible it slipped from my hands, turned a somersault and spilled its contents on the floor: mementoes, pressed flowers, paper money, political ribbons and other papers. Obviously the safe-deposit box! The three of us quickly converted to a pick-up crew and shortly I held in my hand a sheet of paper decorated with writings, designs and colors—blended together in a most attractive pattern. I admired it and as I handed it to one of the girls I said, "There's a work of art for you."

"Vell now, I chust don't know vat dis iss—must be High German—I can't read it. Ven Pop closes his eyes ve'll burn dis trash uff."

"I wouldn't burn anything as beautiful as this," I pleaded.

"Vell, vat gudt iss it ven you don't know vat it gives?"

I began puzzling out the words.

"Vell, if you like it so, chust take it mit you." As she made me the present her face was radiant with a smile, bearing testimony to the deep satisfaction that was hers in giving the pastor something he admired. My affection was likewise kindled and I almost said aloud, "God bless these generous 'Saints.' "

We went down to the kitchen. As I began pulling on my arctics, I thought of the storm and what it would do to the beautiful and delicate acquisition that was mine. I said to Bessie, "Do you have an old newspaper near? I would like to wrap this so it won't get wet?"

Bessie answered, "I 'low ve haf vone someveres."

Again she set off on a search, this time to the cellar. After a while I heard her coming up the stairs. As she turned the door into the kitchen, she frightened me. In so short a time I had never seen so great a change in a person. Her nose was sharp as an eagle's beak; her questioning eyes pierced me through—X-ray eyes they were. "You don't sink it's anysing waluable, do you?"

I don't know how I answered, but I remember saying

to myself, "Well, after all, you gave it to me, didn't you? You old Indian-giver—now the Dutch is showing through —I better get out of here." In no time I said goodnight and was on my way home.

Howard was anxious to see fraktur and I was very happy to share it. The fraktur is enclosed in a trellis design that looks something like a victory arch. The colors are black, yellow, faded green and a rusty red. The letters are strictly Gothic in design and are enriched with glorious lilies, birds, and one squirrel leaping from flower to flower. At the bottom are two fierce dragons—prostrate dragons about to be trampled under foot.

The fraktur reads:

> *Aber ohne Glauben ist unmoglich Gott zu gefallen: den wer zu Gott komen will der mus glauben das Er sey, un denen, die ihn suchen ein vergelter sein werde.*

> But without faith it is impossible to please God; for he that cometh to God must believe that he is, and that he is the rewarder of them which diligently seek him.

The fraktur concludes by giving the reference, Hebrews 11:6; and stating that it was "written in the year of our Lord 1805. To God be the praise." It is signed "D. R."

One fraktur led to another and I went and dug up one of my choice bookplates. I got it at Levi Yoder's—come to think of it, I'm pretty sure it came out of his chicken house. I don't recall the deal. Very likely he made me pin the price tag on it—that was his way—and then just to make sure I was getting my money's worth he would throw in a chicken dinner. I was hardly ever able to get away without "a bite to eat," and if it was mealtime he would draw up an extra chair to the table and make me one of the family. Then before letting me start home he would have to find something for Jim and Daeg. Finally, there would be a basket of tomatoes, or cherries, or apples.

He'd always add, "We can't forget Helen—wonderful wife you have."

Now for the bookplate. The colors are a verdant green and a rich yellow—both loaded with tempera— either egg or cherry gum. The design is that of a heart with tulips growing out of it, while inside the heart is this inscription:

> This spiritual song book belongs to me Maria Larscher . . . born on the sixth day of February, in the year of our Lord 1786.

I am especially fond of this piece of fraktur because it is easy to understand. There are only two outstanding designs: the heart, and the tulips that spring from it. The tulips symbolize the Holy Experiment that got under way with William Penn and the Pennsylvania pioneers. The Quakers came first and soon there followed the many pietistic and sectarian groups, mostly German, in a last desperate effort to escape the tyranny and persecution of the Old World.

For all these groups the tulip symbolized the good life that was shared by the Pennsylvania Saints. This community of brotherly love, as they thought of it, must neces-

89

sarily spring out of the very heart of God. What the fraktur is trying to tell us is that those who first had part in the Holy Experiment knew that it could not succeed except as the hearts of the common people were conditioned by the all-loving heart of the Heavenly Father. Not by evolution, nor by political action, nor by education alone—this good life could be achieved only when men's hearts were warmed and changed by the heart of God.

Because of this conviction the Pennsylvania Saints created a distinctive iconography with the tulip as their chief symbol. The tulip—sometimes it is a rose or lily— is planted in the wilderness by the Virgin Sophia, and, lo, the flower grows and blooms and its fragrance fills the desert air. The Virgin Sophia or the Lady of Wisdom was once prominent in both Jewish and Christian theology. There is the Hagia Sophia Cathedral of Constantinople, one of the greatest architectural structures of the ancient world, built before 600 A. D. The Virgin Sophia was believed by many of the early Christians to antedate the creation and to have had part in it. Sometimes she was thought of as the female element in the Godhead. Having taken part in the creation of life she was associated also with the resurrection of the dead and the gift of life everlasting. This doubtless accounts for the many tombstones in the Dutch country that depict an angelic head set between two wings. It is this Virgin Sophia that plants the tulip, and it is the tulip that gives promise of the life of brotherhood and of life everlasting—the Kingdom of the Tulip.

Frequently it is the lily rather than the tulip that the

Virgin holds in her hands. The Pennsylvania Saints used the lily and the tulip interchangeably in their iconography, and if my Oxford dictionary is on the beam, they were not without justification in doing so. The dictionary informs me that long ago a certain lily grew in Turkey—we're back to Constantinople. The Turks were fond of this lily and persuaded themselves that the full-blown lily looked like the turbans they wore on their heads. Turban was easily corrupted into "Tulband" and "Tulband" into tulip, as you can prove with your own tongue. Call it a lily or a tulip—it doesn't really matter, for they are basically the same flower.

But it's not floriculture that we are concerned about at the moment; it is symbolism. These Pennsylvania Saints knew their Bibles. They knew that in the Temple of ancient Israel "upon the tops of the pillars was lily-work," and they read how certain of the sacred vessels were fashioned "like the flower of a lily." They also gave thought to that line, "I am a rose of Sharon, a lily of the valley." The New Testament confirmed the Old as regards the lily and every Dutchman knew how the Lord Jesus walked through the fields in the springtime and said:

> Consider the lilies of the field, how they grow; they toil not, neither do they spin: And yet I say unto you, That even Solomon in all his glory was not arrayed like one of these.

In the Christian tradition the earlier references are to the lily, the later to the tulip. Call it a lily or a tulip, the Pennsylvania Saints—Protestant, Roman Catholic,

Orthodox—saw in it a symbol of the Kingdom of God as it was to be established here in the wilderness, saw in it the fulfillment of the Holy Experiment.

The lily cult, if one may call it that, is an ancient and respectable tradition. The Greek fathers in the early Church and the later mystics such as Francis of Assisi, Joachim of Flora, and Bernard of Clairvaux transmitted this mystical conception of Christianity to a later group of spiritual leaders including "Meister" Eckhardt and John Tauler, Gerhard Groot of the Netherlands, Jacob Boehme, the inspired cobbler, and Gerhard Tersteegen— we have some of his hymns in our hymnals today—to Casper Schwenkfeld and Johann Arndt, and such Englishmen as George Fox, William Law, and John Woolman.

Joachim Flora in his *Everlasting Gospel* divides all time into three ages:

> The first (age) was a starry night; the second was the dawn; the third will be broad daylight. The first was the image of winter; the second that of spring; the third will be that of summer. The first was the shell; the second the stone; the third will be the kernel.
> The first will bear nettles; the second roses; the third will bear lilies.

There is also Jacob Boehme, the German cobbler and mystic whose influence extended to England and later to the Pennsylvania Dutch land. Some of his books were published at Ephrata. We find him speaking again and again of the "Virgin Sophia," the "lovely Virgin of Paradise," and adding, "In her hand she carries a lily."

Later, when in Europe, the lily cult passed its zenith and began to fade, the purely secular tulip craze took hold. But since by this time the spiritual significance of the lily was fading, and the more colorful tulip was, after all, just another kind of lily, it was natural that such religious emphasis as remained would be slowly shifted from the lily to the tulip. While for most people the tulip was a purely secular flower, not so for the pious separatists and mystics. The Schwenkfelders, Moravians, Mennonites, the more orthodox German groups as well, and the Quakers and Puritans of England continued to think of it as "the sweet-smelling tulip of paradise." The mother of William Penn and her illustrious son made known the significance of the tulip to a large circle of "Friends," and the Pilgrims learned of it as they tarried in Holland and mingled with the mystics there.

The Pilgrim Fathers brought the story of the tulip and the Virgin Sophia to New England, as countless of their tombstones bear indisputable evidence. The early tombstones show the "Virgin" set between wings. There is evidence to indicate that at a later date, when the significance of the Virgin Sophia was lost, her head was transformed into a skull, her wings into the familiar crossbones. Thus the Virgin Sophia—the symbol of that abundant life which is eternal—became a skull and crossbones, the symbol of piracy and death.

There can be little doubt that the Virgin Sophia was best known and best loved amongst the Pennsylvania Dutch. The Virgin and the tulip are constant in their folk art. Then there is Ephrata. Ephrata, Pennsylvania, was inundated with a flood tide of mystical hope. The head of the old Ephrata Cloisters, Johann Conrad Beissel, was constantly speaking about "the fair and noble Sophia, the wisdom of God." Ephrata was not entirely content with its Bible name. It took unto itself a mystical name, also, which was known as "Parthenopolis" the city of the Virgin, as one of my old books affirms on its title page:

The Christian's Duty

To

Render to Caesar the Things that are Caesar's

Considered

With Regard to the Payment of the present Tax of Sixty Thousand Pounds, granted to the King's Use. In which all the Arguments for the Non-payment thereof are examined and refuted: Addressed to the Scrupulous among the People called Quakers, by a Lover of his King and Country.

Philadelphia, Printed; Parthenopolis, Reprinted; by George Zeisiger, M DCC LXIII.

The mystical tradition in its Pennsylvania form constantly depicts the Virgin Sophia carrying in her hand a flower, be it a lily, a tulip, or a rose. She plants this flower in the wilderness in the coldest of the winter at the midnight hour, which is just another way of saying that she, as an agent of Almighty God, intervenes when the human situation appears hopeless.

One is not surprised then if near Christmas time you drop in at a Pennsylvania Dutch Church—Moravian at Bethlehem or Lutheran most anywhere in the Dutch country—and you have the good fortune to hear the faithful sing that sixteenth century hymn, "Es Ist Ein Reis Entsprungen":

Behold a Branch is growing
Of loveliest form and gráce
As prophets sung foreknowing
It springs from Jesse's race,
It bears one little Flower
In midst of coldest winter,
At deepest midnight hour . . .
This Flower, whose fragrance tender
With sweetness fills the air,
Dispels with glorious splendor
The darkness everywhere.

Without some understanding of this Judeo-Christian tradition it is difficult to appreciate the folk art of the Western World, and impossible to make sense of the Pennsylvania Dutch and their "Dutch stuff." Without some knowledge of this mystical hope, how am I to understand the flowers and doves on my Stiegel glass; the tulips on the quilt grandmother pieced; my tole coffeepot, with its gay floral designs done in "August 1818"; the Gaudy Dutch china and the Spatter in peacocks and tulips; the barn signs blossoming so gloriously in the Dutch country; the Virgin Sophia over the doorway at Harmony; the tulip- and Virgin-bedecked tombstones all through the land of the Saints and spilling over into New Jersey, and New England, and Cape Cod; the gay frakturs in so many Pennsylvania homes telling of births and marriages and baptisms, and saying it always with flowers and birds?

Susanna Landis, a Pennsylvania Dutch girl, worked a

sampler in the year 1888. By that time the hope and faith of the earlier Saints were badly corroded, but not for Susanna. She knew and shared the faith of those who first ventured all in the Holy Experiment. Here is what she needled on her sampler:

A blooming paradise of joy
 In this wild desert springs,
And every sense finds straight employ
 On sweet celestial things.
While lilies all around appear,
 And each his story shows;
The Rose of Sharon blossoms here
 The sweetest flower that blows.

Such were some of the things that Howard and I dug up that night when we set about discovering the meaning of the Pennsylvania Dutch tulip. Before going to bed, I told him about two of my New England friends, Wilma and Pierce Beaver, and of their love for things Pennsylvania Dutch. They bought an old dower chest in the Dutch country. It was somewhat on the dilapidated side —had taken quite a beating through the years, and was painted a drab, forbidding brown. Pierce made the necessary repairs. Wilma went to work on the paint, carefully removing layer after layer that successive generations had daubed upon it. Then to their surprise and delight, designs of artistry and color began to appear. By and by, the glorious tulips stood out in all their transcendent splendor and beneath them this bold fraktur inscription:

𝔓enn . . . 𝕶ingdom of the 𝕿ulip . . . 1776

6—Sings Ye Do Togetter

"**B**UTCHERA, Drescha, Boschta, dese are der sings ve do togetter."

The Pennsylvania Dutch believe in each man for himself and each for the other. They are not given to bleary-eyed philosophizing about socialism. Nor are they much interested in tricky economic schemes whereby one is induced to do the work while another reaps the profits. They know they have to invest time and labor in order to make an enterprise profitable and, with this in mind, the Dutch farmer begins at daybreak and keeps going till long after dark.

Everyone who knows anything about it agrees that the Dutch Saint is a hard worker. Sometimes he works alone, more often he works with others. Drop around at a barn about milking time and chances are the whole family will be there doing the milking. Once I saw a little shaver scarcely steady on his feet begging his mother, "Johnnie milk the cow. See, Johnnie squeeze the teat." Johnny did, and the milk gushed into the empty pail with a musical sound.

I thought to myself, "Johnnie, you've hardly graduated from the first squeeze, and here you are on the second." Or watch them work in the fields. It's hardly ever a solo operation. More often the family is working together, and frequently neighbors are also lending a hand, for the hard-working Dutchman is first to say, "Let's do it togetter."

Such operations as butchering, threshing and corn husking demand community participation, and that's the reason the Dutchman will so readily confess, "Butchera, Drescha, Boschta, dese are der sings ve do togetter."

The harvest was over and the cold December winds were beginning to whip down the chimneys. It was butchering time at the Wetzels and Dan was good enough to invite me down for the day. "The Slifers will be dere—you know dem. Ve alvays butcher togetter. It's easier dat vay un more fun."

"Dan, I'll be happy to come. Hope I won't be too much of a nuisance. What time do you get going?"

"Oh, about three-thirty or so. Pretty early fer der Parre, ain't?"

"I'm afraid you're right, Dan; but I'll come—"

"Listen yet vonce. I know vat ve'll do. You cum down fer supper un spend der night mit uns. Den ve can talk over dat Church affair un see iff ve can verk it out so. Yah, you must cum. Den I'll get you uff in der morning."

The supper was a success, as I knew it would be. The Church affair was not so easy to work through. It came eleven o'clock and Dan said, "It makes late already, ain't. Let's to bed go."

The next thing I knew someone was shaking me. "Schtay uff! Schtay uff!"

Then in the next room the same voice, "Schtay uff! Schtay uff! Paul, Paul, uff mit dir. It's time to shoot der pigs."

Dan was a little ashamed of himself. It didn't seem right to awaken a nine-year-old at 3:30 in the morning. But then he had promised, and he would keep his word. Moreover, he appreciated what an exciting day it would be for the kid. He knew very well how Paul had been practicing with his twenty-two rifle for weeks, nor could he forget that the boy had extracted a firm promise he wouldn't have to go to school when butchering day came round.

"Paul, Paul!"

"Yes, Pop, I'm coming."

"You can fill der lantern un get der fires going unter der kettles. Make it burn fast uff. Maybe dis year ve can have boiling vasser by the time der cows are milked un breakfast iss over, ain't?"

"Yes, Pop, I'll get the fires going."

"Gudt, ve don't vant it like last year—der Slifers cum over un made a hell of a fuss cause der vasser vasn't heiss yet."

"Cum, Katie, let's get to der milking; you can get der breakfast on later vile I feed der horses un clean der stable ous. Bring der milk cans. Cum, Parre, you can help mit der cans. I'll take der lantern un der shovel. Did you hear der blow last night? Makes deep snow by der barn door, chust you see vonct."

It was a cold morning with the snow knee deep. The old kerosene lantern sent out its warm, yellow rays, while the crystallized snow reflected the light as though there were millions of tiny bejeweled fairies dressed in every color of the rainbow dancing through the winter night. Just as Dan had expected, a deep drift barred the door.

"Hold der lantern, Katie; hold it chust so, vile I shovel ous," commanded Dan.

"But mine hands iss full," protested Katie.

"Ach now, don't be so dumb. Make your cans down un hold der light." Katie did.

At last the stubborn barn door was pried loose and the warm, moist air—partly cow, partly horse—struck us in the face. Jake entered and looking back confessed, "Feels gudt inside, ain't? It vonders me if it's not near der goose egg dis morning."

The cows were still lying down in their stalls—five o'clock was the usual time for them to begin their day. A few, however, did jump up when we entered and the others Dan encouraged with a restrained kick. When they were all up Dan commented, "Vell, now, you're all uff, ain't? Vat vonders me iss vill you make der milk down?"

"Gib dem der chop, Katie. I'll take der fork un make ready behind." Soon Katie and Dan were each pivoted on a three-legged milking stool, their heads thrust into the soft, warm belly of a cow, and their hands limbering up to the squeeze. There was the swish, swish of milk hitting the bottoms or sides of the pails. The cats, despite the early hour, were also getting awake, several of them standing sleepily on their hind legs begging for a squirt straight from the faucet. Soon we were lugging cans of milk to the milkhouse, while Katie was scraping her shoes and hurrying to the kitchen. Next Dan began feeding the horses and cleaning the stables, all according to plan.

Breakfast was ready without delay, for the men, that is; Katie stood by the stove pitching the batter and taking off the hot cakes. Dan and Paul began hitting the sausage, the syrup, the cakes, and setting a right merry pace. I didn't do badly myself. Katie fell behind.

"Vell," she apologized, "I'm baking dem as fast as I can, ain't? Eat some of der fried potatoes un der creamed beef vile I a little headway make. Un dere's der schnitz pie un der shoofly. Paul, don't you forget—a big dish of prunes for you—dat's gudt fer vat ails you."

But Paul turned a deaf ear. He ran out to put more wood under the kettles. In no time he was back. "Pop, der vasser's boiling good unter der kettles, all but der big vone un dat vone's schteaming already."

"Dat's gudt, Paul. Now let der Slifers cum venever dey vill."

Paul turned his attention to the rifle. Mother spoke up, "Put der gun down, Paul. Ve don't point no guns in der house."

There was a thump on the porch and the stomping of feet—the Slifers had come, all three men. The women would be along a little later.

"Morning, Dan. Hi 'yah, Paul. Cold as hell, ain't? How's der vasser? Steaming yet?"

Paul answered with obvious pride. "It's boiling good. I'm der fireman. Dere vill be no fussing un vaiting dis year."

"Let's go, boys," commanded one of the Slifers. Paul led the way, the rifle in his hand. There wasn't a streak of light in the sky. Jake Slifer turned to Paul. "Gib me der gun; you hold der light so I can see vat I'm shooting at."

"Nothing doing," rebuffed the boy. "I'm doing der shooting. Pop promised me. Ain't that so, Pop? Here, you hold der lantern."

Jake was somewhat amused and even more dubious. He seemed about to say, "Vat, a little schnot-nose like you doing the killing?" but he restrained himself. After all, the boy was a Wetzel, a direct descendant of the Wetzels who hobnobbed with Daniel Boone—quickest and deadliest of the frontier's marksmen—who would turn up their noses at a shot of liquor and turn their backs on a beautiful woman, if they thought they could harvest an Indian scalp or two on the other side of the Ohio. The Wetzels always were killers.

Jake held the lantern. Paul aimed the gun, pulled the trigger, and down came the hog with a thud. Pop Wetzel sprang over the fence, the sticking knife in his hand. One slash and the hog's throat was cut; a geyser of blood shot into the air. Death was bloody and swift. Little Paul must have thought about the expression I had so often heard his pop use, "Bloody as a stuck pig." There was, however, little time for thought. It was a time for action. The gun was reloaded and the operation was repeated again and again until the last of the pigs had started down the long way to the sausage machine.

While the pigs were being killed, the Slifer women put in their appearance. Old Grandmother Slifer insisted on coming along, and so did Mary, though she was terribly plagued with "morning sickness." Already they had transferred most of the soapy, boiling water from the kettles to two huge barrels propped at an angle so that the men could jointly lower and raise the hogs with a mighty heave.

After the scalding came the pulling and the scraping of the bristles, the hanging of the cleaned carcasses under the tripod derricks, the swift movement of the knife in making an end-to-end incision that would catch the envious eye of any surgeon, the removal of the entrails, and on to the butchering house where in greater comfort, thanks to the open fireplace and the dancing, roaring flames, the butchering would go forward with a will.

Grandmother Slifer, bless her heart, took over the dirty work which Mary usually handled. Being in the family way and squeamish, too, the entrails were more than Mary could manage. It was a "drekich" job and soon grandmother's hands and arms would be covered with "Sau Mischt." But she didn't mind. She would see to it that the cleaning and scraping were thorough. She would eat her sausages with relish and a clear conscience, too.

Pop was shaping up the "Hinner Schunka und Rue Maysel"—the hams and spareribs. The Slifers were getting the headmeat into the kettle and putting the sausage grinder together. Then who would show up but old George Schmoyer and his wife.

"Hi-yah, folks," ventured George as he opened the door. "Hattie and me was a sinking you might be needing sum help. Dere's lots of verk ven it cums to butchering, ain't?"

No one was too surprised. Old George was always adept at cutting in whether it were a wedding, a hoedown, or a "butchera." There was a rather cool exchange of glances and greetings. Mary Slifer whispered something about Hattie being "so strubly," so unkempt, and such a "Blabbermaul," which always struck me as a good word for a gossip.

It took Grandma Slifer to set the record straight. "Now George," she said, "It vonders me vy you always show uff at Mittag? Chust to get to der table un make your belly full, ain't? Vel, now dat you're here, get to work. Un, Hattie, go un vash yourself down gudt mit vasser un soap, an den you can crank der sausage grinder. Now chust you go un do as I say."

Hattie went and at least feigned her ablutions, came back and sat down hard and broad. After a while she began turning the sausage grinder more and more slowly, while she turned out her endless queries, quips, and dogmatic pronouncements at a much brisker pace.

"Mary, gone as far as you are, you besser not be butchering, Vy, I lost my last vone in a cake valk." She cleared her throat and brushed back her "strubly" hair. "Did you hear about der Schultz girl, Moses' I mean? Dey say her un long John Brendle ist going to be hitched —Parre Wenrich vill tie der knot. Bet she has to, ain't? Vat it vill give I don't know. If it vas a calf, it vould be a brindle, ain't?"

Hattie's talk was like the weather. "Did you hear about Elder Fogel's vill? Chust sink—he didn't leave a penny to der housekeeper after sleeping mit her all dese years. Said she got hers vile he vas alive. Two farms un all dat money going to the heathern missions. Vell, I chust can't see it, making uff mit der heathern, ven God knows dere's plenty in need right here."

Mary thought it wise to change the drift of the conversation and asked Hattie, "How's your chickens doing?"

"Vell, now, ve're gettin' so many eggs ve don't know vat to do mit 'em. Ach, yah, un half of dem are double eggs, ain't? I blame Pop's big roosters. Ach, did you see how that spritzed me? That dam sausage juice vent right in my eye."

Once Hattie got the bit in her mouth there was no

stopping her. She kept the conversation bubbling about the troubles women have, and how it's fun for the men but the women have all the diapers on their hands. "Glad I have mine raised," she added with a sigh.

She continued, "Ach, it's so much fussing till you get dem housebroke. My kids aren't smart like yours, Mary. Vy look at your Jake, housebroke and in Yale already, ain't?"

Mary agreed, at least in part. "Yes, I have smart boys. Mit girls it's not so easy—you never know ven it vill gif truble, vonce."

"Ach, yah," continued Hattie. "De osser night I seen your oldest vone, Katie, mit dat big lomix of a Blabbermaul—der Horsch boy. Der vone that's so woonerfitzich un fast mit der girls, ain't?"

Katie hesitated about saying anything, but finally concluded that she would have to speak up in defense of her daughter. "Yah, dat's der boy. But my Betty put him in his place I vant you to know. Ven he made to buss her on der porch der osser night, right ous she cum chust so. She said to him right straight, 'Now I vant to tell you somesing. I'm not long big yet un I don't go so much ous. Iss dis fer regular stedy, or chust fer so?' "

That seemed to settle Hattie. Katie stood her ground. When she was sure the issue was concluded she excused herself, rushed to the kitchen and began hurrying the dinner preparations.

A half hour passed and it was time out for dinner. "Cum un essa; cum, essa," Katie called out. Everybody made it hot foot for the spacious kitchen with the long table covered in white and stacked high with all the plenty of the Pennsylvania Dutch. The Schmoyers were first to the table, and George appeared to be reaching for the chicken when Dan flagged him down with the grace. When the prayer was ended, Katie announced, "Hope everybody likes chicken un dumplins—I alvays get filled uff mit der schmell of pork butchering day." Katie had rightly divined the situation. Everybody liked chicken and soon everybody was full of praise for Katie's dumplings. Mary, as she took a luscious drumstick in her hands, remarked, "Not all der old hens are doing as vell as yours, Hattie, or maybe ve are eating some of those over-veight roosters, ain't?"

The boys took up the story, which so easily might have gotten out of hand had not Jake Slifer terminated it by observing, "Besser that vay than ven der woman gets too fett—look at Al Moser, vat back truble he has." Thus the conversation skipped along while the "Fressers" went from meat to dumplings, dumplings to pie, from pie to cake, and finished off with peaches and home-made tapioca pudding.

After dinner, the work was resumed, though for a time at a slower pace, a deduction that would appear to follow naturally if not logically. Slowly the sausage was turned out yard by yard. It was Paul's job to guide the casings ring upon ring, row upon row, round and round the big wooden wash tubs that had been requisitioned for the day.

Most attention was being given to the liver puddings and "ponhaus," or scrapple. Grandmother Slifer measured out the cornmeal, the buckwheat flour, the salt and the pepper, and soon the ponhaus was cooking and bubbling. Said old George Schmoyer, "I like mine fried crisp un brown, un lots of syrup. Ach, zat schmacked gudt."

The butchering had gone off without a hitch. Nearly everything was done except "der vashing dat cums after." Said one of the Slifers, "Vell, it's about time ve go now, ain't? It vill soon be making dark un der chickens must be fed."

Dan Wetzel agreed, and began thanking all his helpers most heartily. "Venever you're ready to butcher, chust let me know. Me un Katie vill give you-uns two days fer vat you've done fer us. Ho, Katie, quick wrap uff a cuple pounds of sausage fer each vone. Give dem a hunk of spareribs, too. Der ponhaus iss too heiss still. I'll see you get some tomorrow. Jake, you go past der Vidow Schultz. I'll send a big bundle of meat. Fer her der going iss hard, ain't?"

The Schmoyers were last to go. Hattie was pleased with the sausage and spareribs but she didn't hesitate to ask for some of the pigs' feet. "My George must have his tsidderlie or dere vill be no sleeping mit him." While the pigs' feet were being wrapped, Paul had an idea. Hattie asked for pigs' feet, why not the tail also? He hurried, got a pig's tail and pinned it to the back of Hattie's sweater. As Hattie and Dan moseyed down the walk, their arms full of butchering, Paul looked at his Dad and exclaimed, "Look at old Hattie, her arm's full of pigs' feet and a 'Sau Schwanz' on her rear!" Pop laughed, Katie laughed, Paul laughed. Then Paul managed a serious turn and with a sober countenance addressed his father, "Pop, next time ve butcher, can I shoot der pigs?"

When it's time to butcher, the Pennsylvania Dutch say, "Let's do it togetter." There can be no question but that it's easier that way and more fun. With threshing it is different, for this is of necessity a cooperative venture, especially among the more conservative of the Plain People, for certain of these Pennsylvania Saints frown upon tractors and the new combine equipment which presupposes them. They may tolerate tractors for stationary work, but in the fields, "Nix, nix, vy zey don't even make manure so." Those who shun tractors, combines and modern machinery are obliged to work with a pool of the neighborhood's manpower.

Such was the stand of Amos Weaver, and no one would try to persuade him otherwise. After all, he got first prize on his wheat at the State Farm Show last year, though because of Church restrictions it was entered in a neighbor's name, and it is said he raised more potatoes on one acre than anyone else in Lancaster County.

This year he was repeating his success story. His barn was full of wheat and oats sheaves up to the rafters, and one wheat field was still in shock. His corn and potato fields were heavy with promise, a forecast of further toil and sweat. Everything about the farm appeared to be stamped with the dollar mark of prosperity.

"Amos, you'll have to pull down your barn un build a bigger vone," advised a neighbor who was first to arrive for the threshing.

"Yah," he answered, "it looks dat vay." He hesitated

a little and added, "But proud, I ain't. It's der gudt Lord dat's showering me mit blessings." Amos stroked his beard and said, seemingly to himself, "Yah, vell, a gudt harvest it gifs, but it's besser to be rich in heaven."

Soon the men were coming from every direction— Mennonites, Amish and a sprinkling of the more worldly kinds who had no special garb. Henner Landis got the oil can and began to lubricate the threshing machine. The sun was coming up with a sizzling sting and every-one was saying, "It'll be a scorcher today." Henner finished the oiling and turned to Amos. "Let's get go-ing," he said. "Every man to his post."

In no time the men had taken their positions. Clayt Yoder would feed the sheaves into the thresher, two men would carry away the grain, the others would divide, half going to the mow and half to the straw shed. Some of the men hesitated about working in the straw. The dust would be terrific, the lack of fresh air, and the sun beating on the tin roof would be almost more than humans could take. Amos Weaver sensed the diffi-culty. He didn't want to order anyone about. He stroked his beard, pulled a handkerchief from his pocket, had it tied over his nose and leading the way said, "Cum on, boys, somebody's got to go in der straw."

Soon the sheaves were being devoured by the mechan-ical monster, while at the same time it was pouring forth at one place the pure, golden grain, and at another place it was coughing and spitting forth endless gobs of dust, chaff, and straw. Once the threshing was under way there was no stopping. From time to time a jug of cold water was passed, and perhaps some light-hearted remark designed to brace up the spirit of both the speaker and the hearer. Otherwise there were no interruptions; only the dinner bell could bring a stay.

Eventually, Martha, a Mennonite maid, ran to the wagon shed and began pulling the bell rope. "Sursum corda, sursum corda," lift up your hearts, the bell seemed to peal. At last the respite had come. Weary men began tossing their hats into the air, dropping their pitchforks, mopping their brows, rubbing their eyes, blowing their noses and drifting in toward the house, for it was "Mittag Essa."

First there were the ablutions. Under the maple trees, on the wash bench, by the pump porch wash basins awaited the men. Buckets of water were there, too, and hanging on the nearby fence were coarse, generous, masculine towels. Soon the men were splashing and blowing, swishing the water about rather like tropical elephants at the close of the day's work. Some got tired waiting their turn. They went to the rain barrel at the corner of the house. After a "dunking" they shook the water out of their beards and then began to wipe themselves dry, leaving, as every woman would expect, the dirt on the towels.

Soon the hungry men were filing into the kitchen and on to the dining room. In reality most of them ate in the living room, for the folding doors between the kitchen and the living room had been opened, creating one large dining hall with one long table stretching from end to end. Everyone was seated; all heads were bowed in a long minute of silent prayer. Then began the "Grosse Esse" or great feast.

On the wall at the far end of the table hung a colorful Taufschein. It was almost fragrant with tulips, and the birds it depicted were of the fancy rather than the "plain" kind. The name "Weaver" stood out in beautiful fraktur as though it had been done by a monk in the Middle Ages. At the other end of the table just above Amos' head was a Haus Segen, done in needlepoint and doubtless of more recent vintage. It began with bold, pleading letters, "God Bless Our Home."

The table was laden with ham, chicken, bologna, dried beef, and the cheese that is so appropriately named "Schtink Kais"; tomatoes, potatoes and gravy, seven sours including "Rot Riewa Oier" or pickled beets and eggs, and seven sweets—cakes, pies, and blackberry mush.

After the sweets had made their final round and not a few tongues had successfully garnered the stray particles lodged in the surrounding beards, Amos arose and in a solemn voice announced, "Wenn wier sott sin, will wier baida," which means, "If everyone has had enough, let us pray." Again every head was bowed and there is reason to believe that every heart was lifted in prayer, for that is the way with Saints. Finally the silence was broken by Amos' voice, "Now, ve must to verk go."

There was no delay. Almost instantly the threshing machine resumed its maddening pace. It was hotter now and the work more arduous. The straw shed was unbearable, but it was unthinkable that anyone should cry "quit." The heat had reached its zenith and some of the men were reassuring themselves with the thought that in another hour or two the threshing would be finished. Then it was that they lowered Amos Weaver to the threshing floor and four men carried the limp Saint out beyond the barn and laid him gently beneath the shade of the first apple tree.

Everyone began to run toward the orchard. Someone called, "Vasser, Vasser, ve must have it quick." One man with a jug rushed forward, "Stand back, I'll spritz him," he commanded. Amos was doused with water, but to no avail. Old Moses Fegley, who practiced "sympathetic medicine" and knew something of the elements of the more orthodox variety, bent low over Amos and felt his pulse. He shook his head sadly, folded Amos' hands, closed his eyes. Then standing erect he took his hat in his hand and said in a firm, solemn voice, "Brother Amos ist gone. Der Lord gave, un der Lord hath taken avay; blessed be der name of der Lord."

The grimy threshermen bowed in silence, their hats in their hands. Before death they stood motionless, helpless, stupefied. Finally Jim Wentz ventured a few words, "Amos vas a gudt man, and a gudt farmer. Vy, look, he raises der best crops in der County."

"Dat iss true," confirmed another. "Vy chust before ve vent to verk, I heard Amos un Ben Shirk talking about vat a good harvest it gifs. Un Ben he quotes from der gudt Buch about der man who had to build bigger barns. How does it go?"

Moses Fegley supplied the answer. "You mean vere it reads:

I vill pull down my barns un build greater; un dere vill I bestow all my fruits un my goods."

"That's right, Moses. Dat's vat dey vas talking. Ve

sought der reaping vas over, but now it's Amos dat's cut down. A bigger barn he don't need, ain't?"

It remained for Jim Wentz to set the record straight, "Yah, but Amos vas no proud man. I heard him say, mit mine own ears, 'It's besser to be rich in heaven.' "

Three days later it was the time of "die Leicht." That day all roads led to the Lower Mennonite Meeting on the Conestoga and they were filled with Amish and Mennonite buggies and wagons. A few of the "fancy" neighbors also ventured forth with their cars. Some seventy carriages followed the death wagon. As the procession wended its way toward the Meeting House and God's Acre, the busy farmers along the road paused in their work and bared their heads while they said to one another, "Amos vas a gudt man, ain't."

The old Meeting House was soon filled. A great multitude was obliged to content themselves with a place beneath the maple trees that stood in a row like a military guard hard by the Meeting. Since the windows were open, those on the outside could also share in the service, and this was fitting, for those Saints who had worked together and prayed together had a right to share their common sorrow. All joined in the solemn worship. Parre Yoder preached the sermon. His text was:

> I will pull down my barns and build greater. But God said this night thy soul shall be required of thee, then whose shall these things be?

When he had finished speaking all the people stood up and sang together as with one triumphant voice:

> Bringing in the sheaves, bringing in the sheaves, We shall come rejoicing bringing in the sheaves.

The things the Dutch do together are sometimes prompted by the hardness of life; sometimes it is the sheer joy of a shared experience that justifies itself. Sometimes it is a blending of the two. It was by virtue of a mixed motive that I was invited to share in the "boschta" at Abe Wentz's. As everyone knew, Abe was "ailing." Annie, his wife, was convinced that "Abe von't get besser till he makes uff his mind un goes to der hospital. Der trusses ain't going to help him, he's got to get fixed mit der knife."

Abe's trouble dated back almost a year when he fell at a barn raising and since that time he had been obliged to piddle around the house and the stables, while Annie did most of the fall sowing and the cutting of the corn, and was now bogged down in husking it, with winter coming on apace.

It was an October moon, a moon that would be full for Halloween. The frost was on the pumpkin and any day might bring snow. Half of the Wentz corn was still on shock. Only a "boschta" could remedy the situation. As we drove into the Wentz's we saw the lighted lanterns moving out to the cornfield. The moon was just coming up; an hour later there would be no need of lanterns.

Everyone was decked out in overalls, men and women alike, except for one or two Mennonite girls whose elders did not approve of girls wearing such "Hosa." At least that was the generally accepted interpretation, although one or two of the boys shared a minority opinion. Everyone agreed that Molly Epstein, Mennonite or not, was boy crazy. Had they not seen her minus her prayer bonnet walking boldly into a Lancaster movie on the arm of Red Fisher from down at the tavern? And had not the story gone the rounds how they had been seen parked in a Ford convertible, and Molly didn't have her prayer bonnet on that time either?

Whatever the motive, whether a girl came designing to trap a boy; or a boy to get a girl; or a man like Pete Miller who came on the lookout for a widow, if possible, one with money; or was it just for the cider, or the sport of it, or to help a neighbor in time of need, the fact is that thirty-seven corn huskers turned out for the Wentz "boschta."

Thirty-seven huskers can shuck out a lot of corn in a night and have a heap of fun doing it, especially if they're Pennsylvania Dutch. These Dutch girls are afraid of neither dishpan nor "boschta" hands. As a matter of fact they lend very little support to the cosmetic enterprise. While two of the men, Jake Hennerschitz and Fred Pentz, were way out ahead in their husking ability, several of the girls, especially Effie Berkenstock and Mary Wiegner, were runners-up.

The moon got brighter and brighter and nearly everyone had "outened" his lantern. There was enough nip in the air so that one had to work just to keep warm. A red ear of corn would, of course, provide the husker, if he happened to be male, an opportunity to warm up, for that privileged him to call the name of a girl, count aloud to ten, and then set out on the chase. What happened when he caught her was determined by three contingencies: his purpose, the distance she ran, the girl. The girl most often called was Molly Epstein.

The husking went along at a clip and doubtless every

ear would have been husked that night had it not been for the baying of the hounds in the woods down over the hill. At first somebody said, "Ach, dey're chust barking at der full moon—vy hounds alvays make so." After a time men's voices were heard down in the woods. That was the give-away. Coon hunters were out and the dogs doubtless had a coon or 'possum up a tree. The temptation was too great for several of the boys and two of them deserted. As they climbed over the fence one of the men let go, "I'll be damned! Chust two faul no goods. Go ahead, get der hell ous mit you."

It was midnight and the working day had ended, but not the "boschta." At the Wentz home there was oyster stew, steaming hot, and as Abe, who had managed the making of it, explained, "Chust a little somesing to take der kault ous of your bones." There were also home-baked pumpkin pies, hot coffee, and "Fasnachts"—the English call them doughnuts, and everybody knows they are just the thing for dunking.

After the refreshments some were about to leave, but Abe pleaded with them, "Nein, nein, you can't go till ve sing a song togetter."

Molly Epstein seized the occasion and led them in singing:

> Two oxen, two donkeys, an old cow that'll moo,
> My father vill give me ven I marry du.
> Some chickens and a rooster, a fat pig or two,
> My father vill give me ven I marry du.

Jennie Schmehl began pleading, "Oh, let's sing 'Clara, Clara, Kommst du Raus.'" Hardly anyone knew it, so

Jennie did it solo in Dutch and in English. Soon every-one was singing:

> *Clara, Clara, kommst du raus de nacht*
> *Clara, Clara, da moon ist arrich hell*
> *Grick, di hoote un jacket on*
> *Sawk di mommie du bleipshd net long*
> *Ich wart fer dich um's eck rum.*

> Clara, Clara, won't you come out tonight?
> Clara, Clara, the moon is shining bright.
> Put your hat and jacket on
> Tell your mother you won't be long,
> I'll wait for you around the corner.

They sang it time after time. Abe commented, "Dat vas nice, ain't?" Then he added, "Chust before you go let's all sing togetter one verse of 'Blest Be der Tie Dat Binds.'" Abe lifted his hand, "Now, all togetter":

> Blest be the tie that binds our hearts in Christian love,
> The fellowship of kindred minds, is like to that above.

"Butchera, Drescha, Boschta"—these are the things we do together.

7—Make Tight Der Reins

"MAKE tight der reins, son. Ven you get on der pike remember it's a colt you have—make tight der reins."

With a wave of the hand the boy and his colt were off to the market in Lancaster. For both of them it was their "solo flight."

Henry Lapp for the first time felt himself to be fully a man and completely on his own. Completely? Well, hardly, for his father's parting words would dog him all day long, "Make tight der reins, son." Going and returning he would "make tight der reins." As he sold the eggs; the home-baked bread, fresh and warm from the outdoor oven; as he put his produce on the scales; as he counted money and made change, he would hear nothing but his father's words. If strangers tried to talk with him; if some city slicker tried to take his picture; he need only concern himself with one admonition, "Make tight der reins."

It was not only the father's admonition that dogged Henry, but his father's prayers. Again and again Jacob Lapp had paused in the day's labors to lift his son on the wings of prayer. Always the petition was the same—that Henry might "standhaft bleiben," remain steadfast, in the way of the Saints. As Jacob Lapp cultivated the corn this was his prayer. Later in the day when as Bishop Lapp, he presided at the funeral of one of his flock, he prayed that all might "standhaft bleiben" and in that petition he included his son, his family—yes, and himself.

Twenty years had gone by since his ordination and he had tried in every way to fulfill those ordination vows: "standhaft bleiben." He could not help but think how the Lord moves in mysterious ways. He didn't want to be a bishop; he didn't want to be a pastor; he was interested only in the good earth and how to cultivate it.

The care and cultivation of souls was not for him. Nevertheless, there was a vacancy to be filled in the ministry and no man of the Church could claim immunity should the lot be his. The congregation voted. Jacob Lapp received five votes and that put his name in the lot. Then came the decisive day. At the close of the long service the Bishop placed eleven Bibles of the same size and binding upon the Table of the Lord. There was one Bible for each candidate—or, perhaps we had better use the term draftee—and in each Bible a little slip of paper, ten of them blank, but one with a verse from Proverbs:

"The lot is cast unto the lap; but the whole disposing thereof is of the Lord."

The congregation knelt for the traditional prayer that asks the guidance of the Holy Spirit in selecting a shepherd for the flock of God. Jacob Lapp held aloof from that prayer. He knew that he was a farmer and that farming was a full-time job. The interruptions and delays that the Lord's work would demand were not for him. Despite his piety, this was a cross heavier than he could bring himself to bear. A prayer came into his mind, he grasped it with the grip of a desperate man and holding to it pleaded with all his heart, "Let this cup pass from me."

The men chose their Bibles; the Bishop opened them one by one. When he came to the paper slip in the Bible of Jacob Lapp, he turned it over and there were written the words: "The lot is cast . . . of the Lord."

Jacob Lapp fell to his knees and in a quivering voice completed his prayer, "nevertheless not as I will but as Thou wilt."

The Bishop announced the decision of Almighty God. Without a moment's delay the ordination was begun. After the long prayers, the admonition to "standhaft bleiben," and the laying on of the hands, the Bishop announced Jacob Lapp to be the new "Diener Zum Buch." Then he gave him the kiss of peace and clasping his quivering hand said, "Brother Jacob, make tight der reins."

Years went by; the good Bishop died. Once again there was a vacancy; once again the congregation voted; once again the Bibles lay upon the table; once again it was Parre Lapp who drew the lot. Immediately he was elevated to the Bishopric. This time there was no one to speak the words, "Make tight der reins." Perhaps it was just as well, for no such admonition was needed. Jacob Lapp was experienced in the ministry, confident and at ease in its narrow ways, and it would be second nature for him to "make tight der reins." The people knew that he would "standhaft bleiben," and in this confidence they rejoiced.

Though Jacob Lapp had been a pastor for some years he had not neglected his farms. On the contrary he had enlarged his acreage while his herds increased and his wealth multiplied. Though he cultivated deep the good earth, he also found time to dig deep into God's Word and into the history and tradition of the Amish Saints. The more he knew about his people's past, the more he believed in making "tight der reins." He had studied

over the old "Meidung Controversy" that caused the
Mennonites to split back in the 1690's, thereby creating
the Amish sect. His sympathies were all with Jacob Ammon in his demand that the Godly shun all who strayed
beyond the "straight and narrow" way. He was Amish
through and through, an Amish Pharisee if ever there
was one.

The Bishop was given to simple questions and answers.
Did it not say in "der gudt Buch": "Come out from
among them and be ye separate saith the Lord"? Did it
not demand that, "A man that is a heretic after the first
and second admonition reject"? Did it not say flatly, "Ye
shall not round the corners of your heads, neither shalt
thou mar the corners of thy beard?"

Jacob had also memorized the words of the old "Dord-
recht Confession." He had written them in his own heart
and was determined through the discipline of shunning
to brand them upon every member of his flock. This was
the mark:

> As regards the withdrawing from, or the shun-
> ning of those who are expelled, we believe and
> confess, that if anyone, whether it be through
> a wicked life or perverse doctrine, is so far
> fallen as to be separated from God, and conse-
> quently rebuked by, and expelled from the
> Church, he must also, according to the doctrine
> of Christ and his Apostles be shunned and
> avoided by all the members of the Church,
> whether it be in eating or drinking, or other
> such like social matters. In short, that we are
> to have nothing to do with him; so that we may

not become defiled by intercourse with him; and partakers of his sins; but that he may be made ashamed, be affected in his mind, convinced in his conscience, and thereby induced to amend his ways.

There you have it, the straight and narrow way as the Amish walked it nearly three hundred years ago, and as Bishop Lapp would have them walk today. They were, and must remain, puritans and separatists, a peculiar and elect people unspotted by the world, a people who would live as Saints, holy unto the Lord. To help them, their beloved Bishop would hold in one hand the Shepherd's rod, while with the other he would "make tight der reins." After all, he had not wanted to be a Parre nor a "Volle Diener," but now that God had drafted him he would dodge no duty nor would he trim the corners of the Amish traditions.

The Bible says "the way of the ungodly shall perish," but the way of the Amish Saint is almost equally perilous. To live in our modern world without benefit of autos, bathrooms, central heating, electricity, telephones, radios, or television is not easy.

Add to this the social inhibitions. Association with the non-Amish is to be kept to an absolute minimum. Public gatherings are to be avoided except for funerals, weddings, Church services, and public sales.

Work is done the slow, hard way. Tractors are not permitted in the fields—such work must be done by horses. The mode of transportation is limited to wagons, carriages and buggies, and the buggies must be without benefit of dashboards. The windows in the home are devoid of all curtains or drapes. No lightning rods are tolerated upon the barns, for this would be an obvious attempt to interfere with the will of the Lord. The cut of all clothing is strictly prescribed. There must be no buttons, and all manner of jewelry and finery are strictly taboo. Even the cut of the hair is regulated for both men and women. The men have their "pot cut" with bangs in front, and on the side the hair falling one inch below the earlobe. There must be no attempt to round the corners either of the hair or the beard. In fact the Amish creed tolerates no rounding of the corners at any point.

To "make tight der reins" was, as the Bishop conceived it, his primary responsibility. He would counsel the young, marry the betrothed, comfort the bereaved, bury the dead—he would do it all with a Bishop's love in his heart and a rod in his hand.

For the most part, the discipline problem would not be great. Most of his people, as he well knew, were zealous to walk in the narrow way. Indeed there were many who would urge upon him an even narrower path and a tighter rein. The Amish, by and large, covet no liberties and desire no changes. What is expected of each is demanded of all. Your house is cold, your oil lamps sputter and smoke, you "go out to the backhouse" when nature insists, you excel in being plain, you travel the slow way, you do it the hard way—but what of it? Your neighbors do the same. In the Amish country there are no Joneses to be kept up with. Everyone walks in the old ways; everyone "bleibt standhaft."

It must be admitted, however, that there appear from time to time certain cracks in this Amish dike. The Amish have their losses, though it is in the nature of a trifling seepage difficult to detect and impossible to measure. While there is some loss in numbers, what is more evident is at times a definite lowering of the esprit de corps. Much of the defection can be traced to the intrusion of the consolidated school. The Amish are quite content with the little old one-room country school. Such a school is equipped pretty much like their homes. But with the newer consolidated schools the situation is radically altered. The children are often obliged to ride in buses; a central heating plant keeps the school warm; electric lights illuminate the rooms; and worst of all there is the mingling of Amish youth with those who make no pretense of being Saints.

How are you going to keep them down on the farm, the older Amish ask, when you let them know all about city ways? It is this worry that sometimes keeps Bishop Lapp awake at night. And what will he do about it? He will "make tight der reins."

Moreover, the Bishop's worries are not always confined to the younger set. There are—as there have probably always been—some of the older Amish who are content to "sit loose." They want to be Saints, but like the illustrious Augustine "not yet." They want to walk in the narrow way, but they don't want to go too far. They are usually careful to avoid any outright violation of the code, but they delight in the misty flats that lie between joyful obedience and arrogant disobedience.

The Amish cannot own autos or trucks. There is one exception. The Wenger Amish have their autos, but they take the "fancy" off them by painting the chrome black

—an indication that members of this little sect may travel with a troubled conscience. Generally speaking, the Amish have neither autos nor trucks, but if they are inclined to play fast and loose with the regulations, they can hire a worldly neighbor to haul them about in his. They are not allowed telephones, but that doesn't keep them from making a nuisance of themselves by constantly using the neighbor's. Even the Bishop is known to have used the telephone, but that was an emergency, to be sure.

I have seen the Amish "kick over the traces," as the saying goes, and do a rather creditable job of it. Some years ago when I was at Rehoboth Beach, Delaware, soaking up sun and ocean by way of a summer vacation, I learned to what extent some few of these Saints violate their way of life. Several families came down from Lancaster County by courtesy of their neighbor's trucks, for which I imagine they put down considerable hard cash on the line, and for a few days they did their best to get along with the people of the world. Several of them made a passing grade.

After some difficulty a friend and I succeeded in engaging one of the wayfaring Amishmen in conversation. We were standing on the boardwalk not too far from the Red Wagon Wheel and right close to the shooting gallery where we watched our Amish friend put down his money, pick up the gun, and bang down the metal ducks as fast as they appeared. My friend, a clergyman, who still dreams in the Dutch dialect, addressed the Amishman in his native tongue. He was obviously surprised and to a degree disarmed—you know how it is when you are in a foreign land and someone addresses you in the vernacular of your home community. Slowly we got round to asking him where he came from.

He answered, "Frum Nei Holland, chust outside Lancaster."

"But how do you get away from the farm?" we inquired. "Who milks the cows?"

"Der neighbors vill milk der cows dis veek. Next veek dey cum down un ve vill milk dere cows."

"But are you allowed to do this? What does the Bishop say?"

Our friend eyed us for a moment. He muttered, "Vat he don't know don't hurt him, ain't?" Mumbling he walked away.

It was fun watching these Amish living up the old adage, "When the cat's away the mice do play." They played, but it didn't come easy. Those big fat women looked a little awkward as they rode the merry-go-round, enjoying, it was obvious, a delayed childhood. It appeared as though their consciences were undisturbed, and doubtless they were right in this, for the Amish are permitted to go to a circus, but only to see the animals. After all, didn't Noah stamp his approval upon the circus when he gathered the animals into his ark?

The Amish seemed to enjoy almost everything the boardwalk provided for the children. When it came to bathing in the ocean they were a sorry sight. The women could not bring themselves to don bathing suits, so they tied down their voluminous skirts with binder twine, as best they could, and waded right out into the surf. They were a prize target for every breaker. The wetter they got the more pathetic they looked—looked for all the world like the kittens I once thought I had drowned in the water trough. The men were a sight, too. Somehow they had managed to dig up some old bathing suits that the moth had spared through the years—the kind with the long sleeves and the tight-fitting, knee-length pants. Thus clothed they ventured out into the ocean where they bobbed up and down while their broad straw hats, better suited to the harvest field than the waves, marked them out like so many sitting ducks on the water.

At the Red Wagon Wheel the Amish did better with their playing. There they enjoyed some snacks, but it was the liquid refreshments that interested them most. The language problem created certain difficulties, but after the proprietor learned that "Schnaps" meant the best whiskey, they got along very well indeed. At least everyone was happy until one night several of the Dutch Saints got a little high and began throwing the dishes around. It was necessary to call the cops. Fortunate were these Saints that their good Bishop Lapp was far away. After all, "Vat he don't know, don't hurt him, ain't?"

The most tragic observation of those Rehoboth days, only they were nights, was seeing several of the Amish girls in their late teens ramble the boardwalk and at the same time make a valiant attempt to keep in the straight and narrow way. One was named Mary, a girl of graceful stature and beautiful complexion. As she threaded her way through the crowds one thought of the blessed Madonna herself. Others saw Mary in a different light and they insisted that in a modern bathing suit she could be a cover girl for any magazine in the land. Her beauty was obvious and striking, and some of the sailors whistled as she went by. But it was hard to keep your eyes on Mary; they were diverted by either her big mannish feet, or the yardage of Amish garb that weighted her down.

It was Mary's last night at the shore and she walked the boardwalk alone. I learned later that she had earned seven dollars selling some of her needlework at the Lancaster Market. Two dollars were left and she determined to spend it all—her final fling. She thought of buying one of the seashell pins. But there were also the custard, peanuts, popcorn, candied apples, barbecues and all the cheap, gaudy knickknacks that the inland Five and Tens couldn't unload. Why, she wondered, did God let the people make so many good and wonderful things? It was the seashell pin, however, that was uppermost in her mind. Before her excursion to Rehoboth, Mary had never seen anything as interesting as a seashell. Chickens, cows, horses, shooflies, apple tarts—these were commonplace, but a seashell was to Mary as wonderful as the stars in the heavens and she coveted that seashell pin as a Hollywood star might covet the Hope diamond. With every passing moment the thought rooted deeper, "I must have dat pin." But what would Pop say, and how about Mom? There was the Bishop, too, who had to be considered. If she bought the pin, well, maybe she'd break a commandment; if she didn't buy it, it would break her heart.

I watched her as she edged closer and closer to the array of pins. She looked at them all; carefully examining one after another. When the clerk approached, she turned and hurried away. Soon she was back repeating the same process. This time her courage equalled her desire; she parted with her money and hurried away, clutching in her hand the one possession of great joy—a seashell pin.

The week at the shore was soon ended, and Mary was back home milking the cows, helping with the tobacco, doing the cooking, and going to Church. After some time she won the backing of her parents and Mary made bold to wear her precious seashell pin to Church. As she went to the "G-may" that day she was the happiest girl in Lancaster County. She kept thinking about the joy of the angels in heaven, as the Bible speaks of it, and she thanked God that some little foretaste was hers. Her joy was real but brief. Even before the meeting began the thought came to her that wearing the pin might be a mistake. Now that her determination had run roughshod over her discretion, the girls were all eyes; the older women all frowns.

She overheard a whisper, "Mary makes gay, ain't?"

Another said, "Chust you vait, she'll go English yet."

The joy of Mary's life became, in the twinkling of an eye, like a dagger piercing her heart. If only she could seize it and pluck it out. Bishop Lapp began his singsong sermon. It was the conventional plea to "standhaft bleiben." Mary thought she detected significant overtones, yet it wasn't so much the Bishop's words as his eyes that troubled her. Those big X-ray eyes were focused upon her; the burning rays were piercing her through and through. "If only I could die"—this was her thought, and for a moment, at least, her prayer.

On the way home from Church she tore the pin from her breast, kissed it, and dropped it by the side of the buggy where the wheel smashed it. She would be done with the pin and never again would she hanker for such gay and forbidden foibles—she would be done with Satan and all his enticing ways, such was her firm resolve. However, the next evening she learned that she was not done with the pin. Bishop Lapp was at the door and he wanted to see her.

"Mary, my daughter," he began with a tone of compassion that belied his true feelings, "it vonders me if you are going fancy. Didn't I see you mit jewelry on at der G-may?"

Mary hung her head and hesitantly stammered her reply, "Yes, Bishop, I am sorry."

"It ain't dat you're sorry dat I vant. You must confess to der congregation un make yourself right before Gott."

"I did wrong. I vill confess. God help me."

"Dat you besser un I vant to talk mit your pop un mon, too. Dey besser make tight der reins around here."

The Bishop turned his attention to the parents. Mary's mother was as submissive as her daughter and volunteered to share a part of the guilt. It was different with Pop. Perhaps he was thinking of the Red Wagon Wheel and concluding that the Bishop was a little too severe with Mary and her sin. When the Bishop began pouring it on, Pop reminded him that there were others who wore fancy pins and that he was reasonably sure that he once saw the Bishop's daughter "mit a fancy pin at der singing."

The Bishop turned pale. "If any of my vomens ever vore a fancy pin it vas because I did not see it." He hesitated a moment while his temper moderated. Then he added, "Yah, vell, maybe dey did vonct, but it vasn't no ornament. It was to hold der dress shut so. Now mit your Mary, it was no pin, for it vas chust on her breast so, for fancy. It vas an ornament—jewerly iss of der devil." As he spoke in a manner ex cathedra he spat on the floor.

Pop argued, but the Bishop could not be budged. At the next meeting Mary must either confess before the congregation or the Bishop would commit her "to the devil un all his angels," and she would become an outcast, shunned by all, even her mother. What her father would do neither he nor anyone knew.

The day for the confession came and Mary, the penitent, appeared in Church looking as crushed as the pin that fell beneath the buggy wheel. She had thought of that way out, for the pike was not far off and the busses went by like lightning. It would be a quick death—but the flames of hell would be eternal. Instead of an eternal hell of fire, she would choose the more temporal hell of the Church; instead of the devil's pitchfork she would elect the Bishop's rod.

After the benediction and the reverent genuflection by all, the Bishop called out Mary's full name and in a loud voice announced, "Dis vicked girl vill now cum forward un make a full confession of her sin before Gott un His people."

Mary came and knelt at the Bishop's feet, confessing, weeping, pleading for mercy. The Bishop was like a piece of statuary; his heart was equally cold. The Church was engulfed in silence except for the sobs of the penitent one. Finally, the Bishop put his hand upon her head. "Mary," he announced, "your sin iss forgiven. Go un sin no more."

Mary had made it right before God; she wasn't sure of the Bishop, nor of all the people. As for herself, the hurt was deep, possibly malignant. Her Pop stood by her, more of a help than she knew. He had arranged for an early schnitzing party the next week, with a view toward "getting Mary ous of her trubles," as he so aptly expressed it. Mary was hesitant about the schnitzing, but with coaxing they persuaded her to have part. The young people came, warmhearted and not only ready to forgive, but to forget. So far as they were concerned Mary's slate was wiped clear when the Bishop said, "Your sin iss forgiven," and they thought of Mary not as a sinner, but as one of the Saints.

Before all the apples were schnitzed, young Henry Lapp, the Bishop's son, seized his opportunity and asked Mary to go with him to the singing next Sunday night. Mary was speechless, and dumbfounded. Finally the words came, "Me, I can't go mit you to der singing."

"Vy, not? Iss some osser feller taking you?"

"Henry, you know vy I can't go mit you. Du bisht der Bishop's son, ain't?"

"I'm Henry Lapp—let's keep der Bishop ous of dis. I'm asking you, vill you mit me go?"

Just as Mary could not say "no" to the Bishop, neither could she refuse his son.

There is no medicine like love. Mary was soon taking it in regular and generous doses. At first eyebrows merely were raised, but before long tongues were wagging and what they were saying did not make for peace and sanctification among the Saints. That Mary had made a mistake, a grievous mistake, as they put it, was known by all. Now that the Bishop's son was "running around mit her" a good many began to talk about "birds of a feather." Others contented themselves with saying the Bishop "besser make tight der reins in his own house."

Henry and Mary were madly in love. People began saying, "Henry un Mary ist going to get g'higher'd, ain't?" But those who were so readily given to loose talk did not know the Bishop who ruled over them and little did they realize how tight he could make the reins.

His own son was first to make the discovery. The Bishop called Henry to the woodshed. As a little boy, Henry had been dressed down more than once in the woodshed, for his father was not one who would spare the rod and spoil the child. Now as a young man about to inherit lands and cattle and wealth and to rule over his own household, he was to be dressed down once more in the woodshed, this time with a certain finality that would hold for this world and the next.

"Son," the cold, venerable Bishop began, "it has cum to my ears dat you're running around mit dat Mary dat makes loose mit Gott un gay mit a pin on her breast. Iss dis so?"

"Father, Mary iss not . . ." He got no further.

"I asked you, yes or no."

"But, Pop . . ."

"Dis iss not your Pop; it iss der Bishop dat iss talking. I ask you again, yes or no?"

"Yes, Bishop," Henry almost gagged on that word. "I love dat . . ."

"Don't spit blasphemy in my face. You are not mixing mit heathens un harlots."

Henry lost his head. "My Gott, man—that's a damn lie."

"Schtop, schtop, you crazy fool. No one can talk to der appointed of Gott like dis. Chust you be careful or he vill strike you det." The Bishop spit on the ground. "If I ever see you mit dat girl I'll lock you ous of heaven un I'll give you over to 'der devil un his angels.'"

Slowly Henry began to come to his senses. He loved that girl and for her he would go through fire and water. But what about hell? After all he was born a Saint and it would not be easy to toss the halo aside. There were the farm and the cattle and the wealth— all his to inherit if he remained a Saint. There were also his people, and the Church, and heaven, too. Slowly Henry bowed his proud neck in defeat and penitence.

The Bishop knew how to "make tight der reins." For Mary the future held nothing but emptiness, pain, and tragedy. Her first love, the seashell pin, was gone— crushed beneath the buggy wheel. Now a greater love was gone, crushed beneath the Bishop's rod. For her there would be no husband and no baby would ever fondle the breast that cushioned that pin. For Mary life would be endless denial, toil, and loneliness—only the distant hope of heaven would remain.

Henry took his punishment like a man. For him there was a way out—there were other girls. He lost no time getting on his way. The more he "ran around" the more expert he became in handling women. He had been serious once and it didn't work out, now he would play the field. It would be love for love's sake, and like the bees he would gather his honey while and where he could.

It was great sport, but Henry slipped. The girl was not his kind. She was a Mennonite, attractive, industrious, pious, one of the Saints, but not an Amish Saint. Time was when the Amish and Mennonites were one, but they had divided over the practice of shunning, the Mennonites being a shade more liberal than the Amish. They had much in common and the Amish knew the Mennonites to be good farmers and Godly neighbors, but because they did not make "so tight der reins" they refused to number them among the elect. Despite all their virtues, from the Amish point of view, the Mennonites were apostates, to be shunned so far as possible. Whenever the question of fellowship between the two groups arose, someone was always quick to quote the Bible: "Can two walk together, except they be agreed?" That settled it.

Henry Lapp knew the regulations forward and backward; the Bishop had seen to that. Nevertheless Henry broke them. This time it was Henry who called his father to the woodshed. Henry had been hard at work shaping timbers for the new barn that was to be his own. The Bishop came to the woodshed slowly and limping, for the infirmities of the years were taking heavy toll of his body; not so his mind. His thoughts were as clean and sharp as ever, his emotions trigger quick, nor had his intuitions failed.

"For vy do you vant me, Henry? Does somesing give truble?"

Henry was grateful for the timely introduction, but

he found it none the less difficult to state the situation.

"Yes, Pop, I'm in truble. It's a girl."

"Henry, I varn you. Ven to me you talk, you talk to der Bishop. If you have somesing to confess, den before der congregation you must go."

"But, Pop, can't you be my father chust vonce?"

"Your father I am. But if it's wrong you have done, you must make your confession before Gott un der Church."

"Pop, I haff to marry der girl."

"Vell, marry her, un make it quick. Who iss dis girl?"

"That's it, you don't know her. She is a Mennonite girl from Lancaster."

"A Mennonite—a heathen, a harlot! So you bring down Gott's appointed to der grave mit sin un disgrace." The Bishop hesitated, then uttered a cry and a prayer. "Oh, Gott, vy must dis happen to der Lord's annointed?" He smote his breast and began crying like a baby. It was too much for Henry. He cried too.

A moment later the Bishop got hold of himself and like Pharoah of old, hardened his heart. "You are going to marry this vench?"

Henry could hardly say it, but finally the words came, "I married her last night."

"You married into der world? Den you have betrayed your birthright un to de world, der flesh un der devil I commit you. Sure as God lifs you vill burn in hell's fire. Take your clothes un get ous mit you. Cum into dis house never again. You shall not lie down here—you nor your vench nor your children. You shall not eat of dis table—it is not to be shared mit devils. Ous mit you; ous mit you quick. Gott help me. I vill yet make tight der reins."

8—Der Battlefield
Iss at Gettysburg

TWO Pennsylvania Dutch farmers were standing on the square in Reading talking crops and cows and weather, including a few grudging remarks concerning women folk and the woes of the world. They fell to arguing about the World War, then in progress, with Dan Stoltzfoos attempting to orient Jake Godshall regarding the entire situation.

"Vell, Jake, I chust hope ve don't get into der var."

"Ach, that can't happen," argued Jake. "Vy der var ist in Europe, acrost der sea. It can't give us no truble."

"Now listen, Jake, that ain't right—dey might chust come over here yet vonct. Now you chust vait un see."

"Don't be so dumb, Dan. Gott in Himmel, if der var makes over here, it von't come to Pennsylvania, ain't?"

"Vy, Jake, it could come to Pennsylvania. Vy not?"

"Vell, Dan, one sing I know, if it cums to Pennsylvania it ain't cummin' to Baerricks County, to Reading."

"Jake, du dum-kup, damned if you know vat you're talking about. It could make var right here."

"Ach, Dan, it vonders me dat you can be so dumb—everybody knows der battlefield iss at Gettysburg!"

Throughout Pennsylvania the Dutch people continue to speak of the "battlefield," having in mind the historic conflict that culminated at Gettysburg, and that despite two great world wars that have intervened, each with its ghastly levy of blood, still "Der Battlefield iss at Gettysburg."

This judgment rests upon adequate supports. The heart of the Dutch country was never really invaded except during the Civil War. The Dutch had a significant part in the Revolutionary War, but with the exception of

Germantown and its environs they never experienced the horror of plunder nor the dreadful ravage of fire in a burnt-earth orgy until the War between the States. Then came the burning of their southern outpost, Chambersburg, and the invasion of their homeland with "foreign" troops penetrating Devil's Den and storming Cemetery Ridge and Old Round Top, all at Gettysburg. The Dutch have a memory like elephants—they can't forget.

There is, however, another reason and one that has enduring validity. It was to Gettysburg and its battlefield that Lincoln came pleading that "government of the people, by the people, and for the people shall not perish from the earth." As we so often hear this concluding line, it is with the emphasis at the wrong place to the neglect of that arresting and global conclusion: "The earth." The question as to whether democracy shall "perish from the earth" remains a burning issue. The end of Gettysburg is not yet.

Just as there are two kinds of Dutch, plain and fancy, so there are two basic attitudes amongst them concerning war and the military. Generally speaking the fancy Dutch are for a strong military, nor have they hesitated to lay down their lives upon the field of battle. When George Washington, the newly appointed Commander-in-Chief, sent out from Cambridge, Massachusetts, a call for volunteers, the first to respond and to present themselves for service were five companies, chiefly Pennsylvania Dutch, from Reading, Allentown, Pottsville, and Lewistown. Again in the Civil War, when Abraham Lincoln called for volunteers, the first to respond were Pennsylvanians, many of them Dutch. The Dutch roster of valor begins with such names as Conrad Weiser, named by the Indians "Tarachawagon," which means "the one who holds the universe in his hands"; Dr. Boda Otto, Senior Surgeon of the American armies during the Revolution; Christopher Ludwig, Baker-General for the Continental Armies. It continues with such Civil War generals as Samuel P. Heintzelman and John F. Hartranft; it concludes with the illustrious names of Carl B. Spaatz, Commander of our Air Forces, and Dwight D. Eisenhower, Commander-in-Chief.

With the plain Dutch the story is different. They are not the fighting kind. Their love of country is no less, but they are unable to forget the promise of the tulip. The dream of a world-wide brotherhood stemming from Pennsylvania, the Holy Experiment, is one that they refuse to surrender. They have the will to live in peace with all men and they actually strive to fulfill the Biblical injunction to "love your enemies."

The Amish, the Mennonites, and most of the other Plain People are conscientious objectors. When war comes they sweat it out on their farms, putting in longer hours and raising additional crops; they volunteer for work in the hospitals; they offer themselves as guinea pigs for all manner of scientific experimentation; and some of them show up in the front lines as stretcher bearers. For their country's sake they welcome the most difficult and perilous assignments. But guns—no. Being Saints they refuse to bear arms. They cannot take life; they do not hesitate to give life.

Though the plain Dutch have declined military service, the fancy have wholeheartedly responded to the call to arms. In the little town of Trappe, not far from the Perkiomen, there stands a Lutheran Church, the oldest Lutheran Church in America. Its massive stone walls and its hand-hewn timbers suggest a stronghold or fort. Redbrown stains on the ancient wood furnishings remind us that it served as a hospital while the American Army was at Valley Forge. The high wineglass pulpit of cherry wood is now mute, but time was when from it came the prophetic and challenging words of Heinrich Melchior Muhlenberg. One of the sons of this Lutheran pioneer was John Peter Gabriel Muhlenberg— and how fitting is that name Gabriel—who when the tide of the Revolution was against America concluded his sermon with these ringing words: "There is a time for all things—a time to preach and a time to fight—and now is the time to fight." He stepped from the pulpit, tossed aside his ecclesiastical vestments, stood before his people in full military uniform, and called for volunteers to follow him to the field of battle. Three hundred men responded at once, pledging their fortunes, their lives, and their sacred honor.

The Lutherans, the Reformed, and the vast majority of the Dutch have established a record of enduring valor upon the field of battle whether in the Revolution, the Civil War, the World Wars, or the lesser ones that have from time to time punctuated our peace.

The Mennonite record is different. For many Mennonites the decision to fight or not to fight is more difficult and distressing than war itself. It is this decision that so often turns children against their parents, neighbors against neighbors, and creates a bitterness more lasting than death.

I remember a Mennonite boy named Lane Kulp who lived and played on the other side of the street. While other children had fun with their toys, especially their toy soldiers, airplanes and guns, little Lane played only with his flags. They were the kind that came from the Five and Dime, just big enough to stick in the ground. All day long, week in and week out, he played with those flags, arranging them one way and then another, grouping them in squares and circles, forming and reforming the lines. In spring the flags mingled with the tulips and waved o'er the crocus; in summer the golden dandelions intruded beneath; in autumn the fallen leaves, and in winter the snow.

One day I stopped at the Five and Ten and bought Lane six toy soldiers and a cowboy gun. There was never a happier kid in the world—in no time those soldiers were on the march and that gun was enjoying its baptism of fire.

The next evening a tearful, shamefaced boy stood on my steps; in one hand was the gun, in the other a paper bag of war-weary soldiers. "I sank you for der gun un soldiers," he stammered. He hesitated, then managed to confess, "I can't keep dem. Pop says guns un soldiers iss against God's commandment. Here dey are; you keep dem." For a moment he lifted his eyes and like a brave soldier looked me in the face. Then he turned and ran behind the lilac bushes where I couldn't see him, but I heard his heartbreak as he sobbed and sobbed.

Guns and soldiers were not for Lane, but he never tired of his flags. Years went by and war broke out in Europe. Lane, now a young man, again came to my door. He wanted to enlist and get into the fight. His heart was set upon the Air Corps. There was one seemingly insurmountable difficulty. He was Mennonite, his people were Mennonites and had always been so. They were adamant in their opposition. His father openly confessed that he would rather have his son dead than the knowledge that "my boy iss a killer."

Lane put his country first. He came to bid me goodbye. I gave him a New Testament. He reached into his pocket and out came six little flags and one toy soldier. "I wish you would keep these for me till I come back. They are some of the flags I used to play with, and that toy soldier, well, he's really yours. Remember the soldiers you gave me? Well, I only returned five of them. Here's one I've kept all these years hidden in the bed tick. I know it wasn't right. Keep him and the flags till I come back."

Finally we came to the words of parting. He bade me a cheery "I'll be seeing you," waved his hand, walked around the lilac bush and was off to war.

Lane never had to take the life of a fellowman. While training as a pilot he crashed and was killed. For a soldier there could be no service in the little Mennonite Meeting House so we were obliged to borrow one of the fancy churches.

The flag draped casket came into the railroad station Monday afternoon. That evening the bell in the village church on the hill began pealing as if it were an Angelus. Villagers and nearby farmers paused in their labors for the bell was telling an old familiar story: God had called home one of his Saints. Every one counted the tolls of the "passing-bell." One clear long toll, then a pause; nine muffled tolls, and another pause; four more muffled tolls—that was the story. The first toll meant ten years; the nine that followed, nine years more. A youth of nineteen years—and one thought of the old prayer with the twist, "If I die before I 'live'." The final four tolls meant four days hence. The funeral would take place Friday. Soon the whole story was known by all and became the chief concern of the entire village. Lane Kulp, the Mennonite patriot, who couldn't take a life had given his own.

Long before the hour of the funeral the Church was filled with plain and fancy alike, for death often wipes out the things that divide us. One more name was added to the roll of those who "gave the last full measure of devotion." Once again the bugler sounded taps and the hills joined in the echo. Once again the stars and stripes were reverently folded and placed into the gnarled hands of a heart-broken mother.

But the last rites were strictly private. That night as the sun sank in the west and the shadows of the evening began to envelop all, I made my way to that fresh mound of earth to perform a solemn duty. Bending low, my work was soon done and when I departed a little toy soldier stood guard and six little flags unfurled themselves in the deepening twilight.

With the Amish the conflict between the flag and the tulip seldom reaches that hour of decision that tries Mennonite souls. The Amish are all farmers and as such they are exempt from the draft. This exemption coupled with their natural aloofness is such that they sometimes hardly know whether the country is in peace or at war. The way it works out for them is indicated by a conversation that took place in the Leacock hardware store near the end of the second World War. An Amish customer complained about the cost of a new scythe which he was thinking of purchasing. "I'm sorry about the price," conceded Hays Pentz, the merchant, "but the war makes everything cost more."

The Amish man eyed him incredulously. Finally he asked, "Ach, I didn't know dat it gives var vonct. Vere now iss der var?"

It requires brave men to win a war. It also requires all manner of arms, materials, and a transportation system to bring the supplies and the men together. During the American Revolution the transportation system was that "ship of inland commerce" known as the Conestoga wagon.

The Conestoga wagon is as Dutch as Lancaster County; as a matter of fact, it's a product of Lancaster County. This wagon, sturdy, long and deep, with a considerable sag built into the middle and an expansive canvas bonnet to defy foul weather, was virtually the only means of transportation during the Revolution. It proved so successful in war that in peacetime this same Conestoga wagon opened the west, made possible the Gold Rush, and survived to play an important part in the Civil War as well.

Even before the Revolutionary War this Pennsylvania Dutch "frigate" drawn by four, six, or eight bell-decked horses and hauling six or eight tons was a means of creating and strengthening the American way of life. When in 1755 General Braddock was preparing his expedition against Fort Duquesne, he had need of 150 wagons and an ample supply of horses. He scoured many parts of Virginia and Maryland, but could round up only twenty-five wagons and not all of them in a serviceable condition. Finally he appealed to Benjamin Franklin for help.

Franklin knew what to do. He advertised at Lancaster:

> Whereas one hundred and fifty waggons with four horses to each waggon, and fifteen hundred saddle or pack horses are wanted for the service of His Majesty's forces now about to rendezvous at Will's Creek and his Excellency General Braddock having been pleased to empower me to contract for the hire of the same I hereby give notice that I shall attend for that purpose at Lancaster . . . and at York.

The Pennsylvania Dutch responded and came forth with wagons and horses in ample numbers. Braddock's expedition was a tragic failure, but not because the Conestogas broke down. When the battle was finished these wagons loaded with the wounded began the retreat and brought their human cargoes safely to the Camp at Laurel Hill. Here most of the wagons were given over to the flames lest they fall into the hands of the enemy.

The toughness of the Conestogas is attested by the expression "I arrived with bells on." Upon the hames of each horse was an arch of pealing, triumphant bells—the prize possession of each wagoner. Next to his wife or his sweetheart he treasured his bells, and as he would protect his loved ones so he would guard his bells, a matter of honor. Since these bells were the ultimate in a wagoner's scale of values there were those who made it a business to collect them by fair means or foul. They were always on the lookout for a Conestoga wayfarer in distress, his wagon broken down, his horses mired in the mud. Having spotted a victim they would extend a helping hand, but the price, what a price, a set of the precious bells! There were few takers, but once in a while a man was obliged to surrender his honor and his bells. Just as our doctors adhere to the Hippocratic Oath so the Conestoga wagoner bound himself by a sacred vow: "I will arrive with bells on," and almost always he made that vow good.

Had it not been for the Conestoga wagons, Washington and his men could never have endured that awful winter at Valley Forge. An army not only marches on its belly, but it also requires huge quantities of food and other supplies when bogged down in the mud. During that winter vast fleets of whitetops, many hundreds of them, manned for the most part by the Pennsylvania Dutch, rumbled along the roads bringing food and powder and lead to the entrenched American forces.

These Dutch wagons also hauled other cargoes of importance. In the spring of 1778 a Conestoga, drawn by four horses and guarded by a full company of soldiers, brought $600,000 in silver, a loan of the French Government, from Portsmouth, New Hampshire, to York, Pennsylvania, the seat of the United States Treasury.

Great as was this contribution of the French, that wagonload of silver is not the most valuable cargo hauled by a Conestoga. A more precious load was hauled from Philadelphia to Allentown in September 1777. The driver was a Dutchman. In fact it appears that there were two drivers and two wagons, for we have the old Moravian record at Bethlehem which asserts that "the wagon broke down here." Perhaps it can be assumed that the precious cargo was transferred from one Conestoga to another at Bethlehem and that a different driver took over. This would account for two bronze tablets erected in the Dutch country:

> Frederick Leaser . . . in September 1777 with his farm team hauled the Liberty Bell from Philadelphia to Allentown where it was concealed in Zion Reformed Church.

> John Jacob Mickley under cover of darkness, and with his farm team, hauled the Liberty Bell from Independence Hall through the British Lines to Allentown.

Leaser or Mickley, either way it's Dutch. The wagon was a Conestoga; the destination, the basement of Zion Reformed Church, Allentown, Pennsylvania; the precious cargo—the Liberty Bell. Thus the bell that proclaimed "liberty throughout the land" was snatched from the metal-hungry Red Coats who would have melted it down and converted it into bullets to maintain their tyranny. Were it not for the Dutch and their Conestogas, America would be without one of its most treasured possessions.

The Dutch provided transportation for the Revolution; they also produced the weapon that assured victory. Have you ever held a so-called Kentucky rifle in your hands? Years ago Henner Landis of the Landis Valley Museum put a so-called Kentucky—in reality a Pennsylvania rifle—in my hands, and as he did he said, "Young man, if it were not for this gun neither you nor I would be alive."

His words I did not then understand. I did have some appreciation for the beauty of that flintlock rifle with its curly maple stock and its brass mountings. The brass patch-box cover with the tulip etching was especially to my liking.

The so-called Kentucky rifle, so named because the frontiersmen carried them into "Kaintuck," is a Pennsylvania Dutch creation through and through. It was first produced at Lancaster back about 1720. The very first ones were made by the Dutch gunsmiths Meylan, Roesser, and Albright and their Huguenot neighbors, Ferree and Lefevre, who were almost equally Dutch in language and customs. These Huguenots of the Pequea Valley, like those of the Oley region, had become absorbed into the Dutch blood stream and were in all respects Dutch, their names excepted.

These Pennsylvania rifles were something new. They were unique in that they had spiral grooves cut into the insides of the barrels. The bullet, a lead ball wrapped in a leather patch, greased and pushed down the barrel with a ramrod, was virtually threaded by the grooves so that following the explosion of the powder it came out spinning. That spin kept it on track of its target—it didn't bounce around in the air as the British musket balls did.

The British with their antiquated muskets were from the first hopelessly outgunned. The Pennsylvania Dutch rifles had a much longer range, were infinitely more accurate, and could be fired more rapidly. From the first the rifle gave promise of victory. The difficulty was that their numbers were inadequate to the task.

What was probably the most important shot of the American Revolution was fired by a Pennsylvania rifle at Saratoga. There at what was then the unbelievable distance of 300 yards a rifleman killed General Simon Fraser. The Red Coats were aghast. At once the British Parliament began inquiring about "those strange rifled arms used with such deadly certainty."

The Continental Congress needed to make no inquiries. It forthwith passed a resolution that "six companies of *expert riflemen* be immediately raised in Pennsylvania." Lancaster County raised more than its share and pushed the State over its quota.

Here were the men and the weapon of ultimate victory, but as yet there were not enough rifles to put the Americans on the offensive. The army went into winter quarters at Valley Forge. Here it was that the great Commander-in-Chief bent his knees in solemn prayer. That prayer was answered as the gunsmiths of the Conestoga and Pequea Valleys redoubled their efforts.

Of course, the war expediters also had their part to play. They lost no time putting pressure upon the Pennsylvania Dutch gunsmiths.

> Resolved, That Mr. Owen Biddle, Mr. Alex'r Wilcock be a committee to agree with William Henry for making 200 Rifles.

William Henry's neighbor, Joel Ferree, was also called upon:

> Resolved that a messenger be sent to Joel Fer-

ree of Lancaster County with a letter from the committee requesting him immediately to complete the Guns wrote for as patterns, and to know how many he can furnish of the same kind and at what price.

Gunsmiths worked around the clock and the forges of the Dutch Country did all in their power to turn the plowshares into Pennsylvania rifles. When at length every American soldier had a rifle in his hands, the British knew it was time to call quits.

Wagons and guns and men were the indispensable ingredients of war when our country was young. The transportation and the weapons have changed, but brave men can never be outmoded. The Dutch country has contributed its share of brave men to the Revolution and to all the wars that have followed.

Its contribution to the Civil War is especially noteworthy. There were those outstanding Generals: John Frederick Hartranft and Samuel Whitaker Pennypacker. And there was Samuel K. Schwenk of Dauphin County who fought in nearly all the great battles and who actually went into the enemy's lines gaining information of their position and numbers. When a party of them surrounded him, intent upon taking him prisoner, he promptly took them captive.

Samuel P. Heintzelman of Manheim was another whose name will live on in the annals of bravery. In the Battle of Bull Run he was severely wounded in the right arm, but he refused to leave the field or even to dismount. A surgeon rode to his side, cut the bullet from the wound, and dressed the mangled arm. In a few minutes the surgery was finished. Heintzelman put spurs to his horse and rammed himself into the thick of the fight. "When," reads the official record, "on that gloomiest of rainy Mondays he dismounted . . . he had been twenty-seven hours on the back of his horse, wounded, worn, and wet."

The Dutch of Pennsylvania have made a magnificent contribution of men and materials to all our wars. They have bled in many of the decisive battles and yet for them it is still true that "Der Battlefield Ist at Gettysburg."

As a Dutchman too young for one war and too old for another, I have never known the terror of battle. If it had been my lot to fight for my country and to fight but once, I am sure it would have been my desire to share in that Dutch expression, "Der Battlefield Ist at Gettysburg."

While a college student I frequently drove past that historic battlefield, but I must confess that what most impressed me were the large roadside signs which read, "Fly Over the Battlefield. Seven Dollars For Seven Minutes." Those signs provoked much sweat and conniving. At last the day came, a November day, but cold as in deepest winter. A cousin joined me in the daring adventure. We drove to the battlefield, located the plane and the pilot.

The pilot was in his warm shack stoking himself with steaming coffee and munching doughnuts. He looked up and greeted us in a rather cordial Pennsylvania Dutch way, "Donnervetter, make der dam door shut. Vat do you vant?"

I answered, "We would like to fly over the Battlefield, sir."

"Mein Gott, men, go un get your heads examined. This ain't no flying weather."

But we were not of a mind to accept his no at face value, for I had long since discovered that the bark of the Dutch is worse than their bite. At that moment I noticed the Boyertown paper crumpled on his desk.

"I'm from down near Boyertown," I confided, and just to make it more convincing I threw in a few Dutch expressions. That did the trick. We began talking about the Boyertown Dutch and the Great Boyertown Fire.

"Some of my people burnt up in that fire," said the flying Dutchman. He hesitated a moment, "My name's Spaatz." We shook hands. Eventually the conversation began to bog down. He put a couple of buckets of water on top of the old pot-bellied stove and poked the fire. "That motor's going to be stiff as hell," he said. "Ach, damm't, I never could say no to a Dutchman."

The other experience came my way some years later when in the capacity of a pastor I called at a home for the aged. Near the parishioner whom I went to visit was a gray-haired lady seated in a wheel chair. She sat erect with a merry twinkle in her eye and a smile that played over her face like summer sunrays falling through moving branches. It was the day before the Fourth of July, in many places the flag was unfurled, and the sound of firecrackers was in the air. We talked about the Fourth, picnics and parades, and of the last of the Civil War veterans. The charming lady in the wheelchair could contain herself no longer and graciously intruded, saying, "I lived at Gettysburg, right on the Battlefield. I was there in the thick of the fight."

I countered, "Why you must have been only a little girl then?"

"That I was," she answered, and she began telling me the whole fascinating story. Her Pennsylvania Dutch father, whose name was Fox, possibly spelled and pronounced Fuchs, was a part-time clergyman in the Reformed Church at Gettysburg, and a part-time farmer. Their farm was in the heart of the Battlefield and as the conflict raged, bullets pierced the house walls of thick stone and mortar. The family was forced to move to the cellar. There they lived, slept, and ate while the battle mounted in fury.

"I was just a little girl, then," she said. "I remember the soldiers came for breakfast, some for supper. Often they were bloody and wounded; some were in gray, others in blue. The chickens couldn't lay eggs fast enough for them, and our hickory smoked bacon soon gave out. We had nothing left but potatoes, and still they came. Oh, I remember it well. Sometimes they saluted; they were always gentlemen. Father or mother said grace, sometimes in English, sometimes in German, and the soldiers shared the food like friendly neighbors. They always thanked mother and some of them took me on their knees. One told me I looked just like his little Katie. Leaving the house they picked up their guns to rejoin the battle. Gentlemen and patriots they were, every one of them."

That Pennsylvania Dutch lady of blessed memory has given me an appreciation of Gettysburg that I could not otherwise have.

She went on to tell how she was denied hearing

the Gettysburg Address "because they said I was too young. But I saw the parade and the big flag go by. I saw Mr. Lincoln, too. He was riding a horse down the street." She hesitated, and then she added, I thought with some qualms of uncertainty, or perhaps hesitant pride, "I saw him waving to the people, and then he waved at me."

Gettysburg is more than an incident in history and more than a monument dedicated to the valor of those who gave the last full measure of their devotion; it is an eternal challenge. Could this be the reason a great man of Pennsylvania Dutch blood, President Dwight D. Eisenhower, maintains his farm at Gettysburg where his eyes are ever fixed upon that battlefield? After all, "Der Battlefield iss at Gettysburg."

9—"Der Parre
Hat Truble, Ain't?"

"**D**ER Parre hat truble, ain't?" With these words I began my ministry in the Church. A Pennsylvania Dutchman passing by paused just long enough to look up and say, "Der Parre hat truble, ain't?"

It was my first day, one might say the first hour. My mother and I—there were no others in the family then—had begun the long day before sunrise. Over roads good and bad, over mountains, beside rivers and through covered bridges we drove from one end of Pennsylvania to the other; for me it was eleven solid hours behind a steering wheel. Those were the days before autos had trunks, and baggage was tied all over the car so that it looked like a gypsy moving van. Parked precariously on top of the spare tire at the rear was a coop of young chickens—after all, every Parre must have his chicken. Halfway and the chickens would have perished from the dust and the heat had I not hit upon a purely Dutch idea. We stopped the car at a gas station, got ice cream cones and those chickens went to it like youngsters at a Sunday School picnic.

Finally we arrived, chickens and all. The parsonage was locked, and every window nailed down, a precaution against tramps, no doubt. We knew nothing about the keys nor did we know where anyone lived. There was nothing better to do than sit on the front steps while we waited and hoped, hoped and waited. It wasn't easy to keep back the tears. Then our hearts were lifted as we saw a man walking up the hill and slowly coming our way. He approached, took one look at us and said, "Der Parre hat truble, ain't?" and went on his way.

Let me add that my first trouble like so many that came

after was of my own making. Had we not arrived hours before the scheduled time, the warmhearted Dutch would have been at the parsonage to welcome us with open arms, and would doubtless have taken us out to dinner and stocked the refrigerator as well.

Troubles are not long in germinating. This is especially true of the more virulent kinds. My thoughts turn to woman trouble, concerning which it need hardly be said that even among the Pennsylvania Dutch the Parre enjoys no immunity. If it happens that he is single and woman-shy to boot, he is particularly vulnerable. Much as he might like to do so, he is in no position to hang out "no gunning" signs. When it is open season you can scarcely blame the fair nimrods if they shoulder their guns and take to the field. There are many good and winsome girls among the Dutch Saints and there is at least one or two strategically poised in every Church Choir. Being a young and single man, I expected trouble from that direction. It came from another.

A woman old enough to be my mother often tarried at the Church door with an apple for "der Parre." Sometimes she held on to my hand until I felt like a drowning man going down for the third time. Always she was urging me to come and visit, enticing me with numerous dinner bids. There was no relief until after my marriage; it didn't take the bride long to break it up. Every time there was an apple she grabbed it. Finally the designing dame gave up and the Parre had peace. Some men boast of their women trouble—not me. I'm like a deep-sea fisherman who has a terrific strike. Excitedly he reels in, high with expectation. He lands it—a loathsome, slimy skate!

A pastor's troubles can be serious. More often they are trivial but of the cumulative kind, like the straw that broke the camel's back. These little troubles have a way of hitting thick and fast. The telephone may catch you in your shorts and if it is one of those days when troubles spawn, you may have a dickens of a time getting your pants on. This is the way things happen among the Saints:

"Hello, iss dis der Parre? Mine baby hast der colic un I can't shush him. Can't you cum now quick vonct un make a prayer?"

You hang up. Again the phone rings. "Dis iss Lizzie Hellfrich. My yungest vone—Gracie, you know—she's going to have a baby. She makes big already, so. Maybe it's Yohn un chust as vell it might be Pete. Now vat I vant to know iss vich vone to pick. My Gracie iss a nice girl un it ought to give a nice man, ain't?"

Before you get rid of Lizzie the doorbell rings. It's Katie Pennypacker. "Did you hear about der vunderful accident last night? Sam Kuhns wrecked his big Buick vonct—ach, it vas vunderful, his wife un four kids vas killed chust like flies."

Again the phone rings. I don't know the lady. I listen while she explains. "Ach, it iss so. Mine Freddie iss liver-growdt un he iss hide bound, too. I took him to der docktor; dat docktor ist so dam dumb he don't know vat liver-growdt iss. Ve passed him shrew der legs of der chair vone vay un der osser. He's no besser. Vat vill I do?"

I am ready to head for the Kuhns' home, but Annie Stritzel holds me up. "Vone sing I know, my cow iss fer-hexed—she gifs sour milk." But that was only the beginning of Annie's troubles. The man who had lived with her twelve years had suddenly moved next door to help out a young widow. "He gifs me no varning, he chust valks ous. Twelf years I feed him un make down der bett, un now vat do I haf to show for it? Like an old hen I sit on der nest un nossnig happens, un now chust you vait, before der summer iss vonct over dat young vidow vill have little vones unter her vings."

Again it's the telephone—my wife relays the message. "Somebody wants to know why you visited the Heffel-fingers yesterday and why you didn't stop next door at the Haldemans. I wrote the number down; told them you'd call." And then by way of rubbing salt into the wounds, my beloved adds, "Don't forget you have that speech at the Oelschlager reunion. And don't forget you must look after the kids while I help out at the quilting— you will have to get the supper tonight."

Weddings are one place where you would hardly expect trouble, but sometimes there is a pang in them for the Parre. Unless he is careful he is sure to get snarled in the red tape and that will mean that his pride will be hurt and he'll end up red as a red-headed woodpecker. There is a heap of etiquette and protocol that belong to a wedding. Plain People are not apt to be interested in it, but the vast majority of the Dutch are not plain and the so-called "fancy" Dutch eat it up. There are sure to be questions about where and how to come in, where to stand, when to kiss the bride, what to do about gloves, when to kneel, where to station the ushers and the at-tendants and the like. The wise pastor schools himself to be ignorant of these fussy considerations, for after all when the chips are down he knows his advice will be discarded and the niceties will be worked out behind his back.

There was at least one exception where I was confronted with a bona fide and pressing inquiry about protocol. It was one of my first weddings and it took place just as the great depression was beginning to lift and the Roosevelt New Deal was getting under way. Many who had waited for years, while selling apples on street corners or trapping in the woods, began to sense the dawn of a better day, take courage, and connive to take a bride.

A Dutch farmer managed to get his "Model T" as far as the parsonage one spring morning when the first robins were busy making their nests. I didn't know the man. We talked weather, and crops, and cows—finally he got down to the agenda:

"Parre, it's been hard making a livin', ain't?"

"You are right about that," I assured him.

"I chust ain't had der money un I'm back mit everysings. My Church dues ain't paid—here's two dollars, I vant to pay uff for der last two years."

I thanked him. He continued, "I cum to get married vonct, Parre. Mary feels to get g'heirat chust now. She don't vant to put it off, so."

I was about to give an affirmative answer. He sensed my approval and continued to carry the ball. "Dat iss gudt, Parre. Ve vill get hitched right now vonct. But tell me— I'm so dumb about everysings un ve vant everysing to be right, so. Dere iss Mary un three of der kids in der auto— vich iss der right vay, baptize der kids or get married first?"

Whether weddings are of the plain or fancy kind, whether they be rush affairs or the kind that move at a

164

smooth and easy tempo, they are apt to generate head-
aches. I remember one of the more fashionable ones where
the people were truly fancy Dutch and there was plenty
of money to throw around. They covered the inside of a
huge Gothic Church with greens and poinsettias so that
you couldn't be sure whether it was a Thuringian forest
or the Florida everglades. They had enough champagne
delivered to the Country Club so that several hundred
guests could take a bath in it, if that's the way they preferred it. Every last detail of protocol and ceremonial was
carefully pinpointed and planned. I was confident there
wouldn't be a hitch despite all the wisecracks about the
groom being late for everything. I overheard someone
say, "Bill, I'll bet you twenty bucks you're late for your
wedding."

The day came and the hour. The bride was there well
before schedule, pretty and anxious as only a bride can
be. The Church organist finished the preliminaries and
now that the hour had struck his eyes were turned in
every direction while his fingers continued a lame im-
provisation by way of camouflaging the agonizing minutes. Everyone was on station awaiting the signal to go
into action. That signal didn't come; there was no groom.
Several times the organist drifted into the opening notes
of the wedding march, but nothing happened. Three minutes, four minutes, five minutes—eternity could be no
longer. Finally the groom came moseying in. What a
relief! Then he spoke to me as man to man. "Pastor,
where is the toilet? I have to . . ." And there I knew
went another five minutes.

Weddings, though they kick up little trouble, can be

terribly disappointing. I have learned that if the groom is the kind who asks right out, "Wie fiel?" or as the English say, "How much do I owe you?" that is a very bad sign. I remember a groom reaching into his pocket and pulling out a twenty-dollar bill along with a handful of change. He asked, "Wie fiel?" put the twenty back and I got the change—seventy-three cents. I harbor no ill toward that Dutchman. Doubtless life had been hard for him, and after all I did know the girl. She was shelf-worn and definitely cut-rate.

I wish I could have that same generous feeling about another wedding involving a twenty-dollar bill. The man was a stranger and I'm sure he wasn't Pennsylvania Dutch, though he was sharp enough to rope in a girl who was one of the Saints. Smart man he was, he got that girl, a dower chest filled with Dutch stuff, and a Berks County farm thrown in. After the ceremony he pulled out a twenty-dollar bill, but just as quickly retrieved it, saying, "Sorry, but I thought it was a fifty. You don't mind a check, do you?"

Well, a check it was and a whopping fifty dollars, too. What a godsend just before Easter! Now the wife could get that new dress and bonnet and the boys could have their new outfits. It would be best foot forward in the Easter Parade. The day after, Monday morning, and the phone rang; it was the store. "Parre, vat kind of a business iss dis? Dat Easter check iss no gudt. I guess you'll haf to reach down in der pocket un make it uff, ain't?"

There is no fool like an old one, or so they say, and I can readily attest it. A couple nearing the seventy mark got together on the green benches at St. Petersburg and decided to make it official with a wedding ceremony back in the bride's Church. The bride went to some length coaching me for the big event by telling of the wealth of her boy friend and how he owned real estate in the West and the South. It was like teasing a hungry dog with a bone.

When the groom showed up he was far from impressive—a little, short, dried-up fellow, carrying in his hands one of the old fashioned horns that served him as a hearing aid. After the ceremony and the kissing of the bride, which I must admit was something of an acrobatic triumph, for she was much taller than he and, moreover, he was obliged to hold both the girl and the horn at the same time, he turned and in a loud voice demanded, "Now Parre, wie fiel?" Meanwhile he dredged from his pocket a bale of greenbacks. My expectations mounted as he removed the rubber bands. He took three bills from the inside and handing them to me said in a voice that boomed through the Church, "Vell, now, I sink dat's about right; ve iss olt un can't live togetter for long, ain't?" Those were his very words. And what was the take? Three dollars!

There is more to being a Parre than weddings. Again and again the pastor finds himself swinging on a fast trapeze between weddings and funerals. As the Dutch say, "Yeder muss schterbe"—Everybody must die. Funerals can be sad, tragic, funny or exciting. One that inclined toward the exciting involved an elderly man of whom I knew nothing. Just before beginning the service the undertaker put his hand upon my shoulder and in his best Dutch manner said, "Parre, if dere's some excitement here today, chust you sit tight. A couple of vomen iss fighting over who vill cover him uff. I haf der cops outside der door—if dey make for a fist fight vonct der cops vill cum in un cool dem down." I felt like the master of ceremonies at a Fourth of July celebration, who doesn't know when the fireworks will go off.

One woman staked her rights on the assertion, "He loved me first."

The second based her demands on the fact, "I'm paying der funeral expenses."

The third, who looked like a member of the High School graduating class, boasted, "He loved me last."

But "Ende gudt, alles gudt"—all's well that ends well—and after the benediction the three wives came forward together, sharing their mutual loss and tears, and together they pulled up the blanket and tucked him in.

Sometimes the most difficult part of a funeral is agreeing upon an acceptable time. A pastor can be only one place at a time; an undertaker has other commitments that hedge him in; the gravediggers have their labor unions and are likewise entitled to some time off. As a general rule burials must take place within certain hours of the day and Sunday funerals are now strictly prohibited, though there was a time when they were very popular. Despite the current regulations, there are some of the Saints, especially the older ones, who continue to hanker for Sunday funerals. As they see it, a Sunday funeral involves no loss of work and it is likely to provide a much larger concourse of mourners. In the old days they counted the buggies and sang about "stars in their crown." The day of the singing and of the buggy is passed, but it is still possible to count autos and that is almost as good

as counting stars. Others go in for counting the hams
or the raisin pies, for it is in this manner that the virtues
of the Saints are reckoned.

I once had a crude family of country folk. The "old
man," as he was always called, and the "old woman" had
five brazen daughters and a silent son of some refinement,
who was obviously an afterthought that didn't really
count. Mother and the daughters had two bad habits:
they all talked at once and each talked louder than the
others put together. The conversation pattern went round
and round like a kite dancing on a string in a March gale
and climbing ever higher into the stratosphere.

Late one night the undertaker called me out of bed.
After a few words of apology he said, "Old man Heffelfritz is dead. They want to bury him on Sunday—I can't
do a thing with them. Will you come down and help
straighten out this mess?"

I couldn't do anything but answer yes. At once I began
steeling myself like a soldier going up to the front. I laid
my plans; first I would dig in for the impending offensive. I did, and it wasn't long in coming. The opening
bombardment was a kind of softening-up operation with
all six guns pumping at me at once. I had to hear how Pop
fell over in the cow stable, how they dragged him to the
door, what a mess he was, how they couldn't get a doctor;
then again how he fell and where he fell and what a mess
he was—round and round we went through that cow
stable. Finally we got down to the point at issue: the
time of the funeral. The battle was joined.

The "old woman" led off: "Mein Gott, Parre, I chust
can't see vy ve can't bury Pop Sundays. Ain't it a free

country?" The five daughters traced the same motif with scarcely a change of syllable, each one saying it louder and faster. There was no opportunity for me to wedge the edge of an answer. The battle swayed to and fro. Soon the first rays of the dawn would be lifting the darkness of the night, but nothing could terminate that stalemate. Finally, old Lizzie Heffelfritz threw in the last hand grenade: "Mein Gott, men, I alvays promised Pop I vould not bury him hot un I'll be damned if I'll bury him stinkin'!"

Troubles are hard to take when you are not responsible for them, but it seems to me that they are even more grievous when you are obliged to plead guilty. I was not trained in the handling of guns; as a matter of fact I was conditioned against it. When gunning season rolled round in the Perkiomen Valley, it seemed as though I was the only creature with such inhibitions. Everyone invited me to go hunting; one man gave me a gun, another fitted me out with high-top shoes. One day I weakened and went out with the Albrights and the Rosenbergers to bag some rabbits, and if I had good luck, a ring-neck or two.

Little Sonny Rosenberger, who had just begun stringing words into sentences, was more excited than anyone else and, though he was much too young to go along, he did his bit by lending his most precious possession, a friendly little black and white fox terrier. Sonny was without playmates—that dog was all he had. Sport, that was his name, was a help and soon he had the rabbits darting madly through the tall weeds and briars. I took a shot at one of those rabbits—it barked and whined in agony. Sport was badly crippled. There was only one thing to do, relieve him with another shot. Having completed that painful task, I faced one infinitely more difficult. There was Sonny to face and somehow I would have to tell him that I shot his Sport.

Evening came and I kept hoping that Sonny would be in bed by the time we returned. It was a foolish thought, for he was first to greet us.

"Did you get anysing?" he asked, directing his first question to me.

Before I could answer I was confronted with a more urgent question, "Where's my Sport?"

I turned a deaf ear. Others likewise avoided the question. There was no escaping it and I tried to answer, but the words would not come. Finally someone in the party pointed a finger at me and told Sonny the whole terrible truth, "Dis man shot your dog."

Sonny couldn't grasp it and again he asked, "Where's my Sport?"

I knelt down and putting my arms about him confessed, "Sonny, my boy, Sport is dead."

He tore himself from me, ran a distance, turned and pointing his finger at me shouted, "You bad man. You killed my Sport."

That boy never forgot, nor would he let me forget. Whenever I chanced to come near him he would point that same finger and say, "You bad man. You killed my Sport."

I don't know how it feels to be found guilty of manslaughter, but I know what it is like to plead guilty to dog slaughter.

In the Dutch Saints there is a streak of stubbornness

that sometimes means that "Der Parre hat trouble, ain't?" Many a time I have seen that stubborn streak make it difficult to hospitalize those in need of institutional care. Only once do I remember seeing that stubbornness work in reverse. A hospital is no place to get stubborn, especially if your neck is broken and you've passed your ninetieth birthday and you have gone through the depression wringer—once a man of wealth, now a creature of poverty. Nevertheless, Louis Schmidt was the stubborn kind and after lying in the hospital through one long winter of torture, they ordered one of those high, hard, goose-neck collars for him and called a taxi.

It didn't work. Louis lived near and he wasn't going home in a taxi. "Un such a collar, dat I vill never vear."

"But you must," they argued. "The doctor has ordered it."

"Doctor or no doctor, dat I von't do. Who's going to order me around, yet? I'm ninety. I don't sink you are going to live dat long. If you make a gudt job un der neck holds uff, dat's gudt, ain't it? If I valk around der corner un it breaks, let it go—I'm ninety un no youngster iss goin' to tell me vat I must do."

Nurses, doctors, officials got nowhere. Finally they hoisted the white flag and said, "Louis, there's the door."

Louis was getting under way when someone rushed up with a paper that had to be signed—some kind of a legal release as I understand it. Louis wasn't signing any paper. He had a good reason, "Mine eyes iss so bad I can't read un vat I can't read I von't sign. Ven I vast a little boy my Mother said, 'Never sign anysing vithout reading it.'"

Again the nurses and the doctors tried, but he couldn't

172

be budged. They brought in a lawyer, the smooth, soft-spoken kind. That didn't work. They called in another noted for his toughness. He failed. In desperation they called the Parre.

The Parre did the best he could—he reasoned, he argued, he pleaded, finally he prayed. That prayer was answered, but not exactly in the expected manner. Louis looked up and said, "Parre, I don't vant to be stubborn. Dese doctors un nurses have been very kind to me, but I can't go against my mother. Tell dem to take der cataracts off mine eyes un ven I can read dat paper I'll sign it."

They operated. Louis read and signed the paper. He walked home minus the "horse collar," as he called it, took over the flower garden and began reading in a chain-smoke manner all the books he could get his hands upon. Ten years went by, he was going strong, and the President of the United States sent him greetings.

Life is like the people in the Dutch country, sometimes gay, sometimes plain. As for the Saints, the plain ones tend to keep to themselves. Occasionally there is a mingling to mutual advantage as at harvest and threshing time, but sometimes this mingling makes for tension, even tragedy.

It was to be so with John and Mary. John was a gay boy in every sense of the word. His people wore no peculiar garb and though no one could sell them short in Pennsylvania Dutch, they preferred the English tongue; John's mother went so far as to show it off with a New England accent which she had managed to pick up while a student at a college in those parts. John was a college boy. His father was going to make an engineer out of him, but John was better at cards and dancing; about the only engineering aptitude he displayed was in handling women.

You can imagine my surprise when one day John brought a girl to see me and she turned out to be a Mennonite. Mary was a plain girl and plainly dressed, but not in Mennonite garb. She explained that she still wore the "prayer bonnet" around home to keep peace in the family but that when she was at college she preferred to dress as most of the other girls did.

Mary went on to explain that she had gone to a college of Pennsylvania Dutch origin with the intention of becoming a missionary. Her pastor encouraged her and she finally mustered the courage to go despite the smouldering opposition of her parents. In college she changed her mind and changed her ways. She decided to become a teacher. She went on to confess her departure from the Mennonite tradition—she loved to dance and she was accounted a clever hand at cards. I thought of the Dutch proverb, *"Die yugent muss ausgedobt habe"*—Youth must have its fling.

We talked cards and dancing and I assured her they could be perfectly innocent pleasures. We talked and all the while I felt that our strip mining conversation was not getting down to the bedrock situation.

Finally John sounded the depths. "Pastor," he hesitated and took another drag on his cigarette, "Mary and I would like to get married but her parents object."

"I can understand that, John. They are Plain People. Have you had a heart-to-heart talk with them?"

"No, they won't talk; won't see me."

"If they feel that strongly about it, I would hesitate plunging into marriage. After all they are Dutch Saints and you hardly qualify."

"I know, but don't you see we've got to get married—Mary's pregnant."

This unhappy business of pre-marital and extramarital relations is one that dogs virtually all classes and conditions of men. The Pennsylvania Dutch—the Saints, even those with pants without flies—are not immune. But let no one jump to the conclusion that the Dutch are loose. While they are less tight lipped and exert little effort to cover up, they bleed, as do others, with shame and guilt. It is unfortunate that we are so constituted that we take for granted the virtues of the many, while we focus our attention upon the few who lapse. The statistics are not at hand and I can't count noses, but I venture that the morality of the Dutch will compare favorably with that of other people, and I'm sure the final report card will give an "A" rating to the Saints.

It was a difficult situation. I urged Mary to speak to her parents and ask them to go with her to their pastor. Then, if she thought it wise, I would also contact her pastor and together we would try and find a way out. By this time Mary was crying. She sobbed, "There, there won't be time for that—Pop knows and he's mad. He's going to lock me in the attic."

The next day I drove over Lancaster way to Paradise, as it is called, but at the moment the name was obviously inappropriate, and I could think of it only in terms of Milton's phrase, "Paradise Lost."

As I drove down the lane I saw Mary's father cultivating the tobacco; her mother, her brothers and baby sister were farther out in the field maneuvering the hoes. I waited until he reached the end of the row and his bay horses pressed against the wire fence.

Then I introduced myself and explained that I had come because of Mary and John. Heinrich eyed me through and through. "If there is anything I can do to help," I began explaining . . .

"Du bisht ein Parre, ain't?"

I assured him that I was—John's pastor—though this I passed over lightly and hastily added that my ability to talk Dutch was very limited. I knew it would be an uphill battle and I wanted to wage it in my own tongue.

"Ich bin ein plain Mann. I ain't gudt mit English. Vy do you cum vonce, to make me more truble yet? Parre Weaver sent my Mary to college un look vat truble it gives—she iss all uffgabindl'd."

"No, Heinrich, I have not come to make trouble. I want to help you and to help Mary. She and John saw me yesterday. I know all about the trouble."

"Mary, she goes to college—it gives a baby un no Papa. For shame she makes herself avay."

"I understand, Heinrich. Could I ask you to take me to the house, I'd like to see Mary."

Heinrich hesitated, then slowly began tying his horses to the fence. "To der house ve can go, but I varn you vonce she ain't goin' to marry John. I vould besser see her in der grave dan gemixed mit der fancy kind."

He led me into the house by way of the kitchen and then up the stairs. We turned—I remembered Mary's words, "Pop knows and he'll lock me in the attic."

We mounted another flight of steps. Heinrich took his keys. He turned the lock and pushed open the attic door. There was Mary hanging by a rope. I reached for a knife but it was no use. I turned to Heinrich to comfort him—that was no use. A few tears came to his eyes; he wiped them away with his blue handkerchief. Finally he spoke, contenting himself with a few words which he repeated over and over again, "It's besser dis vay."

It was a very different kind of trouble that I had with Irvin. Irvin belonged to the fancy or gay Dutch, but with one significant exception, there was little that was gay about his life. He fought with those who went forth in the days of Woodrow Wilson to make the world safe for democracy. Their hopes were frustrated and with many, as in the case of Irvin, they came back shattered in spirit and in health. Irvin had spent many years in psychiatric institutions maintained by the government. While in one of the hospitals he got religion, at least that's the way he put it. Whatever it was, it gave him a fresh start in life and ultimately it opened those locked doors and set Irvin free.

Irvin turned up at our church in Reading. It was hardly his kind—a beautiful, Gothic structure, with the best in music and liturgy, and a Ph.D salted down in many a pew. Judges, lawyers, and doctors were sprinkled through the congregation as so much filler. The rest were schoolteachers and coupon clippers. It was a strictly "uppish" congregation but that didn't bother Irvin. He breezed right in and made himself at home in the front pew. He even brought a girl friend with him. She was the wrong kind for Irvin.

In her purse she carried the picture of her dead husband bedded down in his casket. As she left the Church she never failed to show that picture to the Parre and she also tried without much success to share it with others. Parked in the middle of the aisle with the picture in her hand she was something of a roadblock.

It wasn't the picture of the dead man that bothered the Church elders, it was the ceaseless conversation that she maintained with Irvin during the entire service. It got so bad everyone agreed that something must be done. Finally the elders took the matter in their own hands and determined upon a drastic course. They would gather the offerings at the regular time, bring them to the altar, then two of them would step over to Irvin and his girl friend, take them by the arm, and quickly evict them from the Church. The plans were perfected and carefully rehearsed. As the elders passed the offering plates Irvin failed to toss in the usual quarter. Instead, he carefully placed a ten-dollar bill on top of all the change. Ten dollars! That was too much for those Dutch elders. They couldn't go through with the plan. Confusion engulfed them but it never came near Irvin. Irvin kept his front pew. Surely the Lord must have a way of caring for his own, even the least of the brethren.

With Irvin it was always women that were the cause of his troubles and of mine, too. He was a devout man and an ardent believer in prayer. He had, however, one blind spot. His piety, strange to say, was not typically Dutch; there was too much of the Puritan in it for that. Irvin was especially careful in selecting his friends, both male and female. He insisted that none should swear, nor smoke, nor drink. Toward these vices he was not blind. His blind spot was evidenced in the fact that he had apparently never heard about marriage. He was always wanting a woman, but not the marrying kind. To the lovelorn columns he frequently resorted and from them he would make his selection, always taking care that his housekeeper would be "A gudt Gristian girl who doesn't smoke, nor swear, nor drink."

Katie came. She was that kind. Irvin was supremely happy in his newest acquisition. Again and again he told me, "Katie iss a gudt Gristian girl. She doesn't swear, nor smoke, nor drink. Un she keeps der hous nice, so; un she's a gudt cook—vat fried potatoes un sausage my Katie makes!"

One afternoon the missionary society was meeting at the parsonage. I chanced to look out and there was Irvin free-wheeling on his bike and heading for the door. I didn't want him mixing with the women, so I headed him off in the vestibule. It was a mistake, for the missionary ladies heard everything that happened. Irvin was in trouble, real trouble, and soon the Parre was in trouble, too.

Irvin began, "Parre, I'm in truble. It's Katie. Katie iss a gudt Gristian girl. She doesn't swear nor smoke nor drink. She iss a gudt housekeeper un a gudt cook. But somesings iss cum over her. I prayed un prayed about it but nossing happens. I chust don't have der power to break sthru. Parre, you, I vant to pray, maybe you can get results, quick. Vill you pray now for me un Katie?"

"Sure, Irvin, I'll pray for you, but I don't understand. Just what is your trouble?"

Irvin dropped to his knees. "Parre, Katie iss a gudt Gristian girl, but she von't sleep mit me no more."

There it was: God above, the old missionary ladies in the front room, Irvin on his knees, Katie in her kitchen, and the Parre in between. I tell you, "Der Parre hat truble, ain't?"

10—I Feel To Get G'Heirat

IN the spring the first green shoots hesitate and then push through the frozen earth. The venture is difficult but the urge is irresistible. So it is with love. Since the desire antedates the technique, that first love is bound to be awkward and unpredictable, and that's the way it was with Ben Stoltzfoos and Katie Zook.

Ben began by understanding the difference between roosters and hens, and once he helped Pop take the cow over to Glick's bull. Now Ben was in the eighth grade and school days would soon be over. He could hardly wait—couldn't sit still on the bench, couldn't keep his eyes on the letters and figures that demanded his attention. His eyes were all for Katie Zook and she also had an unquestioned monopoly upon his thoughts. Katie was the prettiest girl in school—Ben was sure of that, and what the other boys said didn't bother him at all.

Once he overheard big Mose Schmucker say, "Katie, her legs iss bowed, ain't?" It made Ben mad and he came mighty near hauling off and giving Mose a punch on the jaw. But Amish Saints don't believe in fighting, and, after all, how could big Mose know anything about Katie's legs—her skirt and apron covered them as though they were under a haystack—and what if they were bowed, what difference would it make? About two things Ben was certain: Katie was the prettiest girl in school and Ben the most miserable boy. Oh, if only he knew how to say, "Katie, I like you," he would be the happiest boy in the whole world.

One Sunday afternoon Ben got up courage to say it. It happened down in the woods where the May apples unfurled their parasols despite the overhanging branches of the white-barked beech. With his penknife in his hands he began telling his love to the world—if not to Katie—by carefully cutting two linked hearts into the smooth inviting bark, putting in the one the letters "K. Z."—only he got the "Z" turned the wrong way—and in the other the signature "B. S." He wasn't quite satisfied, and lest there be some misunderstanding he carved underneath the full name, "Stoltzfoos."

School days ended and there was nothing left for Ben but to slave on the farm from morning to dark, though he did manage to save a little time for daydreaming about Katie. Ben was close-mouthed, as is the way of the Amish, and he shared his secret with no one; but one day when his thoughts were far from his work and he put the wrong harness on the horses and then hitched them to the wrong wagon, his wise Pop said, "Ach, Ben, du bisht so befuddled—everysing iss hinnersfeddersht, back-end-foremost, maybe ven der harvest iss over you can go to der singings. You're big enough to start running around—maybe dat vill settle you."

Ben was most fortunate in his Dad. He wasn't as strict as most Amish are. He never resorted to the whip or the razor-strap. Soft spoken, he seldom said no; and when he did, it seemed to pain him. He was the kind who had more pleasure in opening doors than in banging them shut. Ben knew how lucky he was and outside of Katie there was no one he loved so much as his Dad. Because of his daydreaming he knew he deserved a thorough dressing-down and a severe restriction in his liberties, but Dad contented himself with opening another door.

The immediate effect, however, was far from settling. The very thought of the "singings" was almost intoxicating. It meant that Ben could begin at once actually mapping the strategy of his love. That night when the chores were finished, he walked across the fields to tell Amos Beiler that Pop said he was old enough to "run around" and that he would be going to the singings, and suggested, "Maybe ve can go togetter until I get der hang of it, so."

The singing was at the Gerbers'. While it was Ben's first, his friend, Amos, had been to several; but like some others, he had not as yet gotten round to taking a girl. Ben felt terribly uncomfortable—he knew how to manage in the stable and in the harvest field—but more than brawn was required at a singing and he felt like a fish out of water. There was another anxiety that weighed down upon him: Would Katie be there? As he looked about it seemed as if all the girls from his class in school were there except Katie. Why hadn't he managed in some way to let her know that he was going to the singing? He felt sure that if Katie knew, she would be there. His conscience pricked him; his bashfulness harassed him. If only he had gotten up courage! The barn door opened and everyone began calling out, "Here's Katie"—and Katie it was with her hand in the hand of big Mose Schmucker.

Ben cringed in pain. That fellow who said, "Katie, her legs iss bowed, ain't?" Once again he contemplated that punch on the jaw. There was nothing for him all night but to stew in his anguish. On their way home Amos reported some headway with one of the girls, but Ben was obliged to languish in the slough of despair. The next morning Pop said to Ben, "Vell, son, how vast der singing last night? Nice girls dere, ain't?"

Ben managed to answer, "Ach, Pop, it was chust so."

One thing saved Ben. There was that fraktur that had hung in the schoolroom as long as he could remember. It was an excellent example of penmanship, adorned with birds and tulips. It said, "If at first you don't succeed, try, try again."

That was Ben's way out. A few weeks later Pop and he were helping the Zooks fill their silo. Ben was determined to turn it to his own account. He resolved that this time he would be quick on the draw, for better or for worse. When Katie brought the water out to the men he seized his opportunity, walked right up to her and said, "Katie, vill you go mit me to der singing next veek?"

That next week was a busy one. The harness had to be oiled, the brass ornaments polished, the buggy washed and waxed, the horse's mane and tail braided and put up with fancy ribbon. Ben's unusual zeal was not long in betraying his new interest, and his big brother Dan cashed in on the opportunity to tease him. Even his little sister nosed in with the remark, "It gifs a sweetie, ain't?"

Ben's success at the second singing was not anything to shout about. On the way home he determined once more to tell Katie of his love.

Ben wasn't particularly gifted with the pen—Pennsylvania Dutch he couldn't write because it isn't by nature a written language, and the English he attempted to learn at school was difficult because he so seldom used it. Even the form of his letters was more German than

English. Had it not been for someone else's confession of love which he came upon and copied, he would never have attempted to tell Katie in writing.

However, having a form of words that someone designed, he took them and made them into a beautiful "love knot" that was his own. On a flyleaf torn from the family Bible he executed a balanced geometric design of surpassing grace and much like the tracings in an old Gothic Church window. The background he colored green, the geometrical tracings he left uncolored so that throughout the channel of the design he could write out his message of love. In order for Katie to read the message it would be necessary for her to find the starting point and then to turn it, twist, rotate and maneuver until she came to the end. Outside the knot, in the manner of a floral border, he placed the traditional tulips in all their Dutch splendor; within the knot he bared his affection:

> I have penned an emblem of true love that has
>   no end,
> Crossing, winding, turning, twining in and out
> Never ceasing turning round and round
>   about . . .
> So fairest creature look with pity down
> And do not on an ardent sweetheart frown
> But pardon him that doth thy love desire
> And would delight thy beauty to admire . . .
> When thou hast read this crossing, winding line,
> Be pleased to keep and to preserve it thine,
> Nor let its anxious pleading be denied
> I cross my heart and a true love knot design
>   For Katie Zook

As Katie got out of the buggy that night, Ben handed her the "Gesang Buch" in which he had carefully folded and concealed his "true love knot." And was Katie thrilled? Well, at least she was "pleased to keep and preserve it"—otherwise it would not now be mine.

The Dutch have a saying, "After the ice is broken, it's easy to get your feet wet." Ben found that to be true of love. There is another old saying that relates to horse-racing which points out the advantage in holding the inside of the track. Ben was pleased with the general progress he was making, but most of all he took comfort in the fact that big Mose Schmucker had been nosed to the outside of the track.

Soon all the young fry of the community were talking about how "Ben un Katie iss running around togetter." Once in a while someone ventured the prediction, "Chust you vait, zey'll get g'heirat yet."

The summers came, the winters tarried, and at schnitzings, huskings, and frolics and weddings, too, Katie and Ben were always together. The years went by, Ben was twenty, Katie, eighteen, and love came easier now, and yet there were certain continuing difficulties inherent in the Amish way of going about it. To infringe upon any of these hallowed restraints never occurred to Ben, and, if it had, he would have repulsed every temptation. To have violated one jot or tittle of the tradition of the Saints was not for Ben Stoltzfoos.

Courting at home is difficult for the Amish and yet by reason of their limited social opportunities—no theatre, nor movies, nor Y. M.-Y. W., nor sports, nor nightclubs —much of the love making is confined to the home.

The boy—I hesitate to write it lest all the world go into courting *à la* Amish—the boy is not permitted to call until all the old folks are in bed, presumably fast asleep; then he makes his presence known by focusing his flashlight—don't ask me why they allow flashlights for I can't tell you—upon his sweetheart's bedroom window, or by tossing pebbles against it. If there is no singing or schnitzing or frolic that night, then there is nothing to do but spend the evening together in the bedroom. If it chances to be a long cold winter night, there is the danger of certain complications known as "bundling." Bundling was at one time practiced in parts of Europe and New England and also apparently rather freely indulged in by certain Amish groups. Today it is frowned upon by the Amish clergy and leaders, but still practiced in some instances, because either "it makes so varm" or "it makes so nice." And sometimes it's doubtless not a question of the either-or.

As Ben drove down the Zook lane that night it was very cold. The snow was deep, the moon bright; and as he was about to tie the horse to the hitching post, he noticed that his horse's nose and mouth were enveloped in a mass of hoarfrost. The words came to him about it being "too cold for man or beast," and he decided to unhitch the horse from the sleigh and put him in the stable.

Soon Ben was running from the barn to the house. He would gain a little warmth on the way, for he knew all too well that the Zook home would be colder than the Zook stable. The Amish have no central heating in their homes, nor was there a fireplace of any kind in

Katie's room. With feather ticks heat is a convenience but not a necessity. After all, the women are in the kitchen during the day, the men at the barn; and when night comes they crawl into bed together.

Katie wrapped herself in her shawl; Ben kept his overcoat on. Nevertheless it was too cold for comfort. There was only one warm spot and that was the bed. Katie knew it, but she also knew all too well what the Bishop thought about bundling. She had heard him read, more than once, the admonition from the old "Discipline Book" and while she could not quote it verbatim there was no uncertainty about its meaning. She began recalling the words as best she could:

> With regard to the exercise practiced among the youth, namely that the youth take the liberty to sleep or lie together without any fear or shame, such things shall not be tolerated at all. And when it takes place with the knowledge of the parents and something bad happens on account of it, the parents shall not go unpunished.

Nevertheless one troubled conscience can't forever hold out against two bodies frigid with cold and yet burning with love. They both agreed that at least it would be warmer in bed. Whether it was just because "it makes so varm" or because "it makes so nice," Katie, as she thought back upon it, just didn't know. Was it real or was it a dream? Katie couldn't be sure. The only thing that was sure, next Saturday night Ben came right out and said, "Katie, let's get g'heirat."

These words, "Let's get g'heirat," were the first opening in the dike. That broken dike could never be repaired; now it was a matter of coping with the swift waters, a situation that called for immediate action and for the alerting of the entire community. As the Amish read their Bible they conceive of it as going beyond the specific words, "None of us liveth to himself, and no man dieth to himself," to embrace the assertion that no man marrieth to himself. Which means that the marriage of a boy and girl is never a private or even a family affair, but a public transaction involving the entire community as represented by the Church and especially the Volle Diener or Bishop and the two family groups most immediately concerned. Marriage is a corporate act.

When Ben said to Katie, "Let's get g'heirat," he was not quite playing the game according to Hoyle, and both his request and Katie's response were, strictly speaking, out of order. They could not become a part of the official record, for it is not the young man who proposes—it's the Bishop or one of the lesser clergy that pop the question and nail down the answer.

Ben knew, as many another has discovered, that he had already said too much, and he determined to rectify this rashness at once. Sunday, he knew, would afford that opportunity, for he wanted good Bishop Riehl to be his go-between and the Bishop would of necessity have oversight over the scheduled "Fues Wascha un Nachtmahl," the Foot Washing and the Holy Communion, that would take place at the next meeting.

For Katie and Ben that was a Sunday of transcendent significance. Katie, not knowing Ben's plans, was compelled to play the accompaniment by ear, so to speak. It was a subject that was to be discussed with no one, not even her parents, and Katie was obliged to ride to Church in silence, nursing her anxiety and confining all her fears to herself. Presently they were driving down the Moser lane, carriages before them and carriages behind them, all wending their way to the G-may. As Pop tied his horse near the Moser barn, Katie alighted and began walking toward the house that would be the Church-of-the-day. Mary Yoder came up to her, greeted her in the usual friendly manner, and then leaning over whispered in her ear, "I hear you're goin' to get g'heirat." Katie was dumbfounded. "How could anyone know that?" she asked herself. She wanted to affirm it; she wanted to laugh; she wanted to deny it; she wanted to cry—but instead Katie was like the March winds and she muffed everything.

For Ben the three-hour service was never half so long. As he fidgeted he began to have some idea what eternity meant. The long German prayers read, or to be more accurate sung, from the Prayer Book marched along like a funeral dirge, and the longer silent prayers, on bended knee, made him think of purgatory, or whatever the Amish equivalent is, and also provided ample time to confess his rashness in intruding upon the Bishop's prerogative to ask the question about gettin' g'heirat.

After the prayers, read or silent—the Amish permit no free-lance prayers, believing them to be infected with pride or worldliness, or more likely both—the men in the front room removed their shoes and stockings, the women in the back room did the same, and out came the buckets from under the benches. The men began washing one another's feet. It was Mose Schmucker's turn to wash Ben's feet. As he bent down to do so he whispered, "I hear you're goin' to get g'heirat." They rose together and exchanged the "kiss of peace."

The kiss of peace was hardly what it pretended to be, at least so far as Ben was concerned. He could think only of the kiss that Judas gave. He wanted to haul off and hit Mose on the jaw. Then he came to himself, "Vy, vat's wrong mit me, un right here in der Church? Must be der devil. Vy should I get mad? Maybe it gives congratulations, ain't?"

Meanwhile Katie Zook was having her feet washed in the "G-may" for the last time, or so she hoped. If the Bishop didn't object—he sometimes did, as she well knew—and the other Dieners made no complaint, and her people and his people gave consent, and no one stood up in the congregation and flagged them down at the last moment when the Bishop asked, "Is there anyone who objects to this marriage?"—if all these hurdles were cleared, at the next Fues Wascha it would be Katie Stoltzfoos' feet that would be washed; it would be Katie Stoltzfoos who would exchange the kiss of peace with one of the married sisters. Once liberated, her imagination took free course and she thought of the Bible story about Mary and Elizabeth and how when Mary greeted her cousin Elizabeth with a holy kiss, "the babe leaped in her womb."

After the sermons—the short warmer-upper and the hour-long endurance event—the Eucharistic Prayer and the sharing of the sanctified Bread and Wine—bread that had been baked in the Zook oven by her mother, and wine that had been pressed and aged in the neighbor's cellar—they all knelt as the exhortation to love one another was read from God's Word. They stood for the benediction but at the name of Jesus there was a deep genuflection, every knee touching the floor, all the people bending before the Lord even as the grain when it is about to be harvested bows before the winds.

With the genuflection the formal service ended and the congregation awaited the fellowship of the Love Feast with its easy lunch of bread, butter, jellies, preserves, and a spread that combined in a sticky mass peanut butter and molasses, "Baluunie" and cheese cut in mouthful chunks graced the table in copious manner and there were side dishes of pickles and red beets—the red beets were pickled too—and, of course, there were cups of steaming coffee.

Getting the Love Feast under way took little time, for the white-capped women went to work with a will re-arranging the benches that had served as pews, putting the long table together, spreading the white linen tableclothes —some of them homespun—and loading them down with the plenty of the Dutchland. Their work was made easier by the elimination of all the frills including all saucers, forks, and individual platters or dishes. No Amishman would miss a fork, for even at a sumptuous home dinner he manages to use it only in an awkward way as a "pusher," pushing the peas from the plate to the knife, and knifing them into his mouth. There was a minimum of tools: at each place a cup and a knife and nothing more.

The clergy and the older folks had the benefit of the first table. The hungrier boys and girls would have to hold out to the very end. Three settings would be required to feed the 250 adults that had part in the divine service. The boys didn't mind waiting. They would have an hour or more all on their own. Up in the haymow, down in the stable, and behind the corncrib they could gather to talk over the girls and to exchange the facts of life. For Ben it was one of his last lessons. Soon they would push him off the gangplank and he would be deep in the matrimonial waters to sink or to swim.

The first table was a long time slowing down to a stop. There were visiting clergy, something that didn't happen too often, and they spent a good deal of time exchanging the secrets of the trade. Jokes and laughter also intruded, for that was the way with one of the visitors, big-hearted Bishop Aaron Esh, beloved of all his people. Another Parre, Daniel King from down by Bird-in-Hand, also had some appreciation for the lighter side of life. Bishop Yoder, who came in from Ohio, was on the stern side, but since it was his first visit to Pennsylvania, he was full of questions, all of which took time.

Bishop Riehl did his best to make the guests feel at home. Several times he repeated, "Now everybody pitch in un help yourself—ve pass nossings." And that's the way it was, everyone using his knife like a dagger to spear his food. They speared the bread, spread it, and mouthed it. They speared the cheese and with their teeth pulled it from the knife. Fingers, a knife and a cup—these were their tools. Poor Bishop Yoder wasn't accustomed to the Lancaster County simplicity. Some couldn't keep from laughing as they watched him spear a red beet, shake off the red vinegar, then transfer it to his fingers and eat it like a squirrel nibbling on a nut. But he was not long in getting the hang of Lancaster County etiquette and soon he was planking his red beet, juice and all, on the white linen tablecloth, right in front of him, cutting it into pieces, and knifing it to his mouth.

For the second setting the tablecloth would be covered with large red splotches, but it would take more than beet juice to upset an Amish stomach. By the time Katie and Ben were accommodated at the third setting, the tablecloth was a slaughterhouse red. That didn't bother them—Katie had wrung the neck of many a rooster and Ben had long practiced obstetrics in the cow stable.

Finally the Love Feast came to an end. There were the shaking of hands, the friendly greetings of parting friends, and the men went out to hitch their horses. Soon all—men and women, boys and girls—were on their way to their homes and to their work; all except Ben and some of the clergy.

Ben went to his buggy, did some adjusting of the harness to kill time and allay suspicion, meanwhile keeping on the alert for Bishop Riehl. Finally the Bishop and his helpers emerged. Again Ben felt like that schoolboy who had something that must be said but who lacked the courage to say it. The January blasts cut him through and through—this time there was no feather tick to take the edge off the weather—but Ben didn't mind the cold; instead, he mopped the sweat from his brow.

The Bishop began untying his horse. Ben walked up to give him a hand with the blanket. This was the moment, and Ben seized it as a hungry dog seizes a bone. "Parre," he said, "I feel to get g'heirat. I vould like to get hitched to Katie Zook. Vill you look into it?"

Bishop Riehl stroked his beard and answered, "It vonders me vy you stayed so long single. Der gudt Buch says it's besser to be g'heirat. I vill look into it un tell you vat it gifs. Now, chust you vait."

Ben felt better; at least the Bishop had not "put his foot on it," as he sometimes delighted to do. Moreover, Ben knew that the fat was now in the fire and he was thankful that the Bishop had a reputation of letting no grass grow under his feet. He would make himself scarce around the house for the next couple days; it would be better that way when the Bishop came to talk it over with his parents. He would keep away from the Zook home, too. The days were short and the Bishop might be there, even after dark. The most difficult thing about a verdict is the waiting that is so often a prerequisite. Two inescapable questions confronted Ben as he waited day and night: When would the answer come, and what would the answer be?

Saturday night just as Ben finished milking the last cow, who should step into the stable but Bishop Riehl. After a curt but friendly greeting that took in the entire family, he turned to Ben and said, "Young man, it's you I vant to see."

Ben knew what that meant. He followed the Bishop to his horse and carriage. The Bishop began untying the horse, and again Ben began unbuckling the blanket to fold it. Suddenly the Bishop put a hand up on Ben's shoulder, "Young man, you're going to be married. It makes for a big vedding. Ve vill publish it at der next G-may."

At length the day for the solemn announcement came. The usual three-hour service concluded in the usual way

with the benediction and the genuflection. Then everyone was seated for the announcements. Inasmuch as most
of the weddings take place in the late fall, only a few of
the young folk surmised that this might be the day when
"Ben un Katie iss announced." The usual announcements
ran their course—a funeral, a quilting, a meeting about
the new school regulations. The Bishop paused, and with
added solemnity announced: "If there are no objections,
Benjamin Stoltzfoos un Katie Zook vill be united in marriage."

There were no objections. Ever so many people were
overheard saying, "So Ben un Katie gets g'heirat. It makes
for besser dis vay, ain't?" Ben had taken care so as to be
seated on a bench near the door. He didn't tarry for the
usual handshaking but bolted out and sprang for his horse
and buggy. By the time the young people came out shout-
ing, "Ben's goin' to get g'heirat," he was on his way down
the lane and bent for the Zook home and his beloved
Katie. He lost no time in reaching his destination; the first
time he had dared to go there in broad daylight. Katie was
awaiting him, for it is customary for the girl to absent
herself from Church the day of the announcement.
With her was a girl friend, Levina Weaver. Soon the
older Zooks came home from Church. Katie's Dad took
Ben by the hand and wished him God's blessing. "Now
you're my son, ain't? Un I'm your Pop."

There was no time for ceremony; it was time to eat.
Ben was assigned his place; all were seated; all bowed in
prayer. Then as the meal got under way they recalled and
reviewed every incident of the day. Ben told how he was
too nervous to eat breakfast; Katie told how she smashed

the cream pitcher on the cellar stairs; Pop how he forgot to feed the horses; Mama Zook how she started to Church with her stable shoes on. Then they recounted the service, what this one said and that one, pausing to fondle every unusual word or incident. There was laughter and there were tears, but they pressed on to what lay ahead.

First to be attended to was choosing the wedding guests and the plan and timing of their invitation. They counted the uncles, the aunts, the cousins, the closest friends of the bride and groom and they began considering the nearest neighbors. In no time the list was beyond the two hundred mark, and there were so many more who ought to be included.

"But ve ain't got room fer so many," cautioned Papa Zook.

"Ach, vell—dey only get g'heirat vonct, ain't?" That was the way Katie's mother looked at it.

So they compromised and agreed upon 198.

It was Ben's responsibility to invite all the guests. This time he would not attempt to say it in writing; not because he was convinced of his literary limitations, but because no Amish Saint would show up at a wedding without being extended a personal invitation by the groom. Here, as in so many instances, the Amish keep to the old ways, for inasmuch as there were wedding invitations before there were mailmen to deliver them, the Amish spurn the services of the mailman in so important an event. They do it the old way.

The wedding suit was also to be provided. Fortunately Ben had bought the material—a charcoal gray—and had stowed it away several years in advance saying, "It vill

shall we say sung, for all Amish sermons are done in the old way, more or less intoned—by the Bishop himself. Like most of the sermons, he knew this one by heart, for it was nearly twenty years since he began preaching it. It was an old sermon, no one could say how old, for it had been handed down among the clergy, generation after generation, as was also the way with their Gregorian chants. In fact it was so well known by the people, that should the Bishop hesitate or stumble, someone would quickly help him on his way.

Despite its traditional character, the sermon was interesting, especially that part from the Apocrypha in the old Saur Bible that tells how Tobit went in quest of a wife. Even though he took an angel as a guide, his father admonished him before his departure:

> Beware my child of all whoredom, and take first
> a wife of the seed of thy fathers, and take not a
> strange wife, which is not of thy father's tribe:
> for we are the sons of the prophets.

Then followed the part about the love potion, a potion that was also good for the opening of a man's eyes, and how the angel addressed Tobit:

> Behold, take her to thyself after the law of
> Moses, and lead her away to thy father.

A few concluding words and the marriage was ready to be forged.

There would be no organ music or instrumental music of any kind. There would be no wedding march to the tempo of "Here comes the bride." There would be no orange blossoms or bridal veil, no flowers of any kind, no jewelry, no cosmetics—no externals, to captivate the eyes or the ears. The Bishop simply asked the bride and groom to arise and stand before him. He announced their names in a solemn manner and for the last time asked them whether they had changed their mind. Again he inquired whether anyone present had any objection. Then addressing the young couple he said, "Since I hear no objections, ve vill proceed."

God's House was swallowed up in silence. Before the Bishop stood Benjamin Stoltzfoos trembling in his carefully tailored Muthze. By his side was Katie Zook, beautiful as is the way with brides, and beautiful despite the lack of flowers, jewelry and cosmetics. Her garments were the proper garments made of the costliest materials and carefully tailored. For the last time she was wearing the black cap, the white cape, and the white apron starched "chust so." Hereafter she would always be dressed as the married women are: a blue or black cape, a black apron and a white cap. There would be one exception, one final exception. When at the end of her life the time came for "die Leicht," Katie's wedding garments would be taken out of the dower chest and once again she would be dressed as a bride, a bride of her Blessed Lord in the heavenly and eternal world.

Again the Bishop spoke clear and to the point: "Benjamin, do you take Katie as your lawful, wedded wife . . . until God shall separate you by death? If so, answer, 'I do.' "

Then to the bride: "Katie, do you take Benjamin to be your lawful, wedded husband . . . to cherish and obey him until God shall separate you by death? If so, answer, 'I do.' "

After the answers, the Bishop took Katie's hand and placed it in the hand of Benjamin and said:

"By the authority of the Church and the Commonwealth of Pennsylvania, I pronounce you husband and wife. 'The blessing of God Almighty, the Father, the Son, and the Holy Ghost, be upon you and remain with you forever. Amen.' Depart in peace."

Everyone genuflected, bowing low at the name of Christ. A parting hymn was sung. The congregation was seated while the clergy and the bridal party gathered their wraps and made their way out. Soon the happy throng was hastening to the Zook home, where there would be hot coffee and a glorious wedding dinner to crown the festive occasion.

Arriving at the Zooks', the women hastened to the house while the men unhitched and stabled the horses. There wasn't enough room below, so they parked some of the horses on the spacious threshing floor. With this chore attended to, the men also hurried to the house. When all the preparations were completed, the Bishop announced, "Dinner iss ready."

In no time they all assembled in their proper places, for the Amish insist upon a pattern of conduct that must be maintained "because it's always been dis vay." So the older women took their places, the girls theirs, the men, the boys, the song leaders, and last of all, at a little elevated table, the bride and groom and the bridal party. Then said the Bishop, "Let us all be seated; let us pray."

After the silent grace there was no time lost in getting

to the business of the afternoon, that of eating. Course followed course and platter after platter went round and round: turkey, chicken, ham and escalloped oysters, potato filling, bread filling, three different gravies, mashed potatoes, candied sweets, pickled cabbage, all kinds of cheese, fruit salad, tapioca pudding, peach pie, cherry pie, raisin pie and about forty home-baked cakes, some with icings heaped high and anything but "plain."

When everyone was too full to eat, it was time to sing. All turned to the seven hymns that are sung at every wedding feast, beginning with the three Gregorian Chants that antedate the Reformation. So they continued singing and waiting—though there was considerable nibbling going on between choral responses—until the grandfather clock struck four.

Four o'clock and the last round of the wedding festivities began. Despite the cold the young folks took over on the barn floor singing and dancing. They did all the fast, hard steps, swinging their partners with gusto and maintaining a brisk enough tempo to keep reasonably warm.

This last round was for the young folks only and would continue far into the night. But before the older people could actually begin the journey home, their participation in one final ceremonial act was required to make the marriage effective. All the unmarried men together with the the nervous groom lined up on the outside of the barnyard fence, all the married men on the other side.

At a signal all the young blades fell upon the one who was deserting their ranks. They fell upon Ben, seized him as though they would tear him apart, limb by limb. Big Mose Schmucker grabbed one leg, Amos Beiler who took

Ben to his first singing, the other, and with a mighty heave they lifted him high, Muthze and overcoat and all, and flung him with violence over the fence as though he were a big bag of garbage. The young men shouted, "Over der fence iss ous." The older men caught him and eased his fall.

Now Ben Stoltzfoos could raise a beard and sleep with a woman, even on hot nights. And though he would not be tempted to say, "It makes so varm," he might say, "It makes so nice, ain't?"

After the older folks had seen Ben safely across the fence, they began hitching their horses, lighting their lanterns for the warmth they would give, and starting on the long way home and to the chores that awaited them.

11—Harmony on the Connoquenessing

ARMONY is a golden word. It reflects beauty, melody, and tranquility. There is a Harmony that is different, one that you may chance to find upon a Pennsylvania map in the Butler-Beaver County area, tucked away in a pocket on the banks of the Connoquenessing. There it lies in the mud flats like a fossil that once was alive but now something to be kicked around by antiquarians only. Harmony is like an egg with two yolks, for it is separated from Zelienople—never mind the Greek in that name, it's as Dutch as Harmony—by a narrow alley called Division Street. In terms of life, Zelienople has an edge on Harmony, for the Perry Highway runs right down the main street. It is a community of rustic charm and it has its own distinctive Dutch heritage, but so far as the outside world is concerned Zelienople is nothing but a bottleneck and a headache, as any week-end traveler will most emphatically affirm. As for Harmony, well, outsiders would most certainly agree to let it stagnate in oblivion.

It is one thing for an outsider to go down Harmony way, but it is different when you think of it as your home. To be truthful, neither Harmony nor Zelienople was my home, but that is about as close as a neophyte can hope to approach Chestnut Ridge on the old "Harmony R. F. D. 39, Box 18." I was born there because I belonged there; at least the Dutch half of me belonged there, and one of my earliest memories is the Virgin Sophia chiseled into the old stone doorway above the Harmony wine cellar. Many a time I asked about that strange yet angelic figure, but no one was able to name it or tell its meaning. The Harmonists had put it there.

Why? Nobody knew.

That a peculiar people once lived in Harmony was common knowledge. It was attested by the old clock in the Church tower with its one hand pointing out the hour—minutes didn't count. It was enough for the first Harmonists to know the hour. Indeed it was enough that the watchman knew the hour. At the close of the day it was his duty to make the rounds calling out, "Again a day is past, and a step made nearer to our end; our time runs away, and the joys of heaven are our reward." At three o'clock in the morning the same voice announced, "Again a night is past, and the morning is come; our time runs away, and the joys of heaven are our reward." That old clock is not alone in its testimony, for there is the graveyard with its high stone wall and revolving stone door. Above that door is a German inscription telling that, "Here Rest a hundred members of the Harmony Society who died from 1805 to 1815." Within the walls there are neither mounds nor tombstones; it is not so many individuals but a part of the Society that slumbers there in the democracy of death. On every hand are brick buildings of old world architecture and beneath some of them repose deep-vaulted wine cellars. Harmony was different and in a way Harmony remains different—different because those who settled there in 1805 were a different people.

George Rapp, a German pietist and visionary, determined to have a part, albeit a delayed part, in William Penn's Holy Experiment. He came to Baltimore in 1803 with his son John at his side and $800 in his pocket. Shortly afterward he gobbled up 6,000 acres of wilderness along the Connoquenessing. He soon wrote back to Germany advising his co-laborer, Frederick Reichert, that the journey was long and perilous and that no one should be urged to come. That did it. Soon three ships were on the Atlantic carrying pious pilgrims to Western Pennsylvania where it would be their task to push back the wilderness and establish a Christian community where all would be shared and all would be "harmony."

The Harmonists lost no time in laying out the town and putting up their houses, each one set in a quarter-acre lot. They also built barns, a grist mill, a brewery, a distillery, a blacksmith shop, a tannery, a dyer's shop, an inn, and a Church. The structures, though built to last for all eternity, were thrown up with such haste you might have thought they were a pre-fab job. They built a bridge, too, a covered wooden bridge 220 feet long over the Connoquenessing. It was a bow-string structure that long served the Harmonists and their successors. All that remains are the blueprints, but they are enough to throw our modern engineers into a tizzy.

Organizing the people took a little longer, but George Rapp went about it with a will and in a relatively short time everyone had become putty in his hands. He determined that it was to be a religious-communistic adventure with all the property and wealth vested in his name. The people were bound to obey the rules and regulations which he, for the most part, decreed, and he in turn was obliged to supply all their wants, providing an all inclusive social security for this world, and for the world to come the assurance of heavenly bliss.

Father Rapp was their leader, physician, judge, ruler,

and priest. He was an exceedingly devout man who was obsessed by many of the same mystical ideas that had captivated the heart of William Penn's mother and of the first Germans who settled Pennsylvania. He was also convinced that the world was near its end and that Harmony, Pennsylvania, must soon give way to a heavenly "harmony." For him the end of the old world meant the beginning of a life of brotherhood upon the earth—the time of the tulip and the rose. In the time of the rose, he believed, the Christ would come again, the Temple in Jerusalem would be rebuilt, and all the Saints would return to Palestine. Having in mind this early return to the "New Jerusalem," he purchased instruments of navigation and had the youth instructed in the use of them. He also stowed away huge quantities of gold and silver which he determined to take to Jerusalem where they would be used to furnish and beautify God's House. Into the stone side of a high, conical hill, he carved a wide seat, from which he could oversee all. While he waited with his eyes ever turned expectantly toward the heavens, he would, in the short time that remained, do his best to make genuine Saints of all his followers and establish a temporary "harmony" on the banks of the Connoquenessing.

Despite the shortness of the time, as Rapp conceived it, he was determined to do all in his power to enrich each passing moment, both for his own sake and for the sake of his people. Consequently he encouraged, at every turn, the advancement of the arts and sciences. The love of the beautiful was a part of his nature and the Harmony he built was to be a place of beauty. When flowers were available, they kept the covered bridge decked with the blooms of the garden. Not far from Rapp's seat he constructed a garden labyrinth of shrubbery and flowers and nearby he maintained a botanical garden stocked with all the known herbs that could be acclimated. Plants, flowers, and fountains, these were commonplace in Harmony. It hardly seems necessary to add that the air was filled with music. Everyone was encouraged to play an instrument and hardly a sunset fell on Harmony without eliciting the accompaniment of music and song. In reality Harmony was just what its name claimed it to be.

While there was time for culture, there was no time for leisure. Rapp was of the conviction, and his people shared it, that man's chief enemies are leisure and sex. These evils he determined to eradicate. It was easy to take care of the leisure problem—work them from sunrise until bedtime and work them hard. The people were to be saved from their sins by hard work. Early in the morning the women went forth to the fields following the plow, or with sickles in their hands to work side by side with the men. The boys and girls went to school in the forenoon. In the afternoon they were obliged to work —they tended the sheep, labored in the shops, loaded brick and shaped timber. Everybody worked, for there were vineyards and orchards to plant and care for, cattle to tend, harvesting to be done, hides to be converted into leather and rye into whiskey, food to be garnered and stored, flax to be made into clothes, the virgin soil to be subdued, and community life in all its intricate complexities to be established and maintained.

They started with nothing but the good earth and the

drive of the Saint. Four years later they produced 6,000 bushels of corn, 10,000 bushels of potatoes, 5,000 bushels of oats, 4,500 bushels of wheat and a like number of rye. They sold some of their surplus food. The barley they converted into beer and 1,600 bushels of rye they sold or consumed in liquid form. Their livestock increased also —they had horses, cattle, hogs, poultry, and sheep. They brought to America the first merino sheep, paying a thousand dollars for a single ram. Within ten years they cleared and fenced 3,000 acres of land, planted 2,000 apple trees and fifteen acres of vineyard. After ten years they estimated their wealth at $220,000—no mean sum for the year 1815.

When one considers their amazing industry, it is natural to think about Rapp's stone throne high on the hillside. From this vantage point—now a lover's paradise— the Patriarch was able, with the aid of a glass, to watch all his workers up and down the Connoquenessing Valley and with his huge megaphone to bellow his commands. They toiled as men who knew that the eyes of the boss were upon them. George Rapp might well go down in history as America's first efficiency expert.

It was easy to abolish leisure—one might think it would be more difficult to abolish sex. Difficult or not, George Rapp did it. That there was an instance or two of cheating is rather well established. Be that as it may, sex was almost as rare in Harmony as golden slippers.

It is doubtful whether Rapp could have succeeded in this unorthodox venture had it not been for certain mighty theological convictions which his people shared with him. The Virgin Sophia reminded all the Harmonists that God had a feminine as well as a masculine nature. God, as they understood him, was both male and female. Since man was made in God's image it followed that man must be a creature of dual sex. In theological parlance we are back to Adam and Eve, or perhaps it is just Adam. When sin took place in the Garden of Eden, man's sex balance was disturbed and everyone became imperfect, even defective—some became males while others became females. These yearning, burning, frustrated creatures looked about them and saw what fun the animals had. They began playing the same "game"—sex in paradise. Despite the antiquity of the "game," Rapp, somehow, was able to persuade his followers that sex was subhuman and downright sin. He maintained that after a continuing period of total sexual abstinence all would recover their dual sexuality, and life would go along without the benefit of sex-play between men and women. Marriage he permitted, but he saw to it that the women slept on one floor, the men on another. He may have been generous enough to let them hold hands but of that I am not sure. In Church the men sat on one side and the women on the other. Why they got married I don't know, but it couldn't have meant much.

Ten years and Harmony was everything the name suggested. The community prospered in every way except one—there were no babies. Harmony's whiskey, wool, wine, indeed, its over-all prosperity, made it widely known and in that time Pittsburgh was located as "twenty-five miles beyond Harmony."

Harmony was established; the Harmonists could look back upon the hard days and look forward to days of ease and happiness—a foretaste of that heavenly harmony desired by every heart. Then the incredible happened. George Rapp sold out—sold everything except the burial ground, sold it for less than half of its value, a measly $100,000. At least, that was the cash payment. Whatever he got on the balance—and historians are divided on whether he got anything—must have come years later.

Rapp had decided to go West. He had in mind to venture into the wilderness of Indiana and there establish a New Harmony. This he did. Again his people prospered, again it was harmony on earth except that scores died of malaria. Ten years went by and once more Rapp decided to move. He sold New Harmony to the Owenites, returned to Pennsylvania and built Economy at Ambridge on the Ohio River, fifteen miles from the original Harmony. It was their last move; they prospered to the end, which came inexorably—no one devised a method of having babies without sex.

The Harmonists were in many respects like the other Pennsylvania Dutch who are so prevalent in southeastern Pennsylvania and are found in island groups all through the State. They were almost a carbon copy of what took place at Ephrata where fifty years earlier the "solitary" brothers and sisters lived the monastic life and reverenced the Virgin Sophia. In their celibate life, in their musical achievement, in their love of the beautiful, in their practice of fraktur they were like the Saints of Ephrata. With the Harmonists the Virgin Sophia was more given to the planting of the rose than of the lily or tulip. The rose—often it was a golden rose—became the symbol of their spiritual aspirations. Nevertheless they also knew the meaning of the tulip. Before me is a *Harmonisches Gesang Buch*, the official hymnal of the Harmony Society. This copy was printed in Allentown, Pennsylvania, by Heinrich Ebner in 1820. That was before the Harmony Society got their own press going. This particular copy contains a beautiful fraktur plate, rich in color, heavy in tempera. It is as beautiful as anything that was done at Ephrata. At least a dozen glorious tulips ornament the text which reads:

> Dieses Gesang Buch Gehoer Carolina Stundermaierin, In Harmonie.

The Harmonists made Harmony what it was intended to be. After they left, the "real" Dutch came. Rapp sold out to Abraham Zeigler of Lehigh County and in came the Mennonites. The Zeiglers, Beavers, Boyers, Musselmans, Eicholtzes, and Moyers rushed to take over the Harmonist's beds while they were still warm. Like the Harmonists they were Saints and hard workers, but they were not the kind that would turn their money over to someone else. Not the Zieglers or Zeiglers, I know them.

Soon the Mennonites were building their stone Meeting House with the pulpit down in the middle and the pews like chicken roosts on the four sides. The land adjoining the Church they set apart as their burial ground. Abraham Zeigler is buried there and as peaceful as any of the Saints, but that must be difficult for one who aspired to be a second Father Rapp. Time was when Abraham had set himself up as banker, storekeeper, miller, brewer and boss. Now he rests beneath the blackberry bushes in a tranquility sanctified by the singing of birds.

The Mennonite influx brought to Harmony all the cultural benefits of the pure-blooded Pennsylvania Dutch. The Dutch language took over and in came Schnitz un Knepp and Shoofly pie, Lebkuchen, Ponhaus and all the business about "Fressen un Essen." They also brought their Saur Bibles with them, John Baer's Almanac, and Hohman's *Long Lost Friend*. Harmony became the Western outpost of the Pennsylvania Dutch.

The Harmonists came first, the Mennonites second; my people came later. The Brenners found the going increasingly rough in Germany; it was especially difficult for them because they lived near the French border. There was constant tension and either war or the threat of war hung ever over them. French and German soldiers ravaged the land. In order to have something for his hungry family old Heinrich Brenner had to hide his potatoes in the manure pile.

The Brenners were slow in making up their minds, but they finally decided to try for a better life in Pennsylvania. They crossed the ocean in 1832 and then by means of the newly constructed Erie Canal and the road that Perry had gouged out of the wilderness painfully edged their way toward Harmony. Along with them came the Burrys, Mullers, Buhls, Stamms, Staufers and a host of others. Here they became neighbors of the prosperous Mennonites and of the small groups of Lutheran or Reformed people who had preceded them. The Mennonites, however, continued to be the dominant group, leavening the whole loaf; and soon Harmony was Dutch to the core.

Two generations later and a skinny, premature baby

came through, though the doctor wasn't able to make it because of the deep snow. The baby was hastily wrapped in cotton, put in a dresser drawer and pushed near the kitchen stove. He was given a very special diet—cow's milk and whiskey.

The baby soon became a boy, but still the diet was something special. He was put on Butler County's staff of life—buckwheat cakes for breakfast. The buckwheat cakes began about Thanksgiving time and continued through to Easter without a break.

Doubtless the constancy of the diet was dictated by the nature of the cakes, for the first ones were made by a "starter" of potato water. Thereafter each day some of the batter was saved to become the starter for the next day's cakes. It was much like pioneer days when they kept a little fire on the hearth at all times because it was too difficult to start one from scratch.

In those days Harmony was a rather isolated community. Bananas and oranges came in for the holidays only. Our meat was pork and beef, mostly pork, but for one memorable exception. Each spring the Dindingers imported a barrel of fish from Lake Erie. What excitement there was when the fish arrived! The word went round by courier, "The Dindingers have fish." Soon everyone was heading for Dindingers with either a basket on his arm or a bucket in his hand.

At length the Harmony Short Line made it possible for our people to go places, even to far away Pittsburgh. Only a few took advantage of this boon, for after all when you stay put long enough you don't become the traveling kind over night. Though most of us failed to get to the city, the city came to us.

Perhaps the most interesting contact with the outside world was by way of a walking department store. That department store came to our house three or four times a year and what an exciting event it was. A neighbor would come running or the telephone on the wall would set off its noisy gong. However the news got through, it was always good news, thrilling news: "Westermann is coming."

Several times I was fortunate in spotting him far down the road, but one couldn't always be sure whether it was a load of hay or Westermann, the walking department store, on his way. In winter it was easier to sight him, for his mountain-like bundle of merchandise stood out clear against the towering snowbanks. But whether it was snow, or rain, or mud, knee deep, Westermann got through.

In summer Westermann displayed his merchandise on the porch; in winter he spread it out over the kitchen floor. There it was in its vast and baffling array: frying pans, work plants, gum shoes, safety pins, needles and thread, cough syrup, syrup of figs, Father John's, men's shirts, ladies' skirts, suspenders, garters, pocket knives, dollar watches with a guarantee attached, wedding rings—booties for the baby, corsets for the lady of the house, and "the finest of pants for the missus." Only Atlas could equal Westermann in the load upon his back.

If Westerman chanced to come at mealtime, there was no embarrassment, for he carried his groceries with him and no one could tempt him to depart from his diet which consisted of hunks of black, hard bread and one onion, both of which he carved with his pocket knife. He carried his own tin cup and sometimes he would allow us to fill it with plain black coffee. At noon time Dad and he would get to talking Dutch. Westermann's languages were legion, in keeping with the merchandise on his back, but somehow it seemed the language of his preference was Pennsylvania Dutch.

At length the outside world broke through in mass, and sleepy Harmony was disturbed and awakened when the drillers came, greedy for gas and oil. Soon every little stream and rivulet was covered with oil, for as the wells came in by the dozens and then the hundreds they spouted their liquid wealth high into the sky. Harmony was drenched in oil. In those days old, dingy streets were suddenly illuminated with blazing torches of gas that poured over the upturned buckets and stretched their flaming fingers high toward the heavens. They burned day and night; there was no way of turning them out. These prodigal days lasted only a few years. When the punch-drunk attitude gave way to a more conservative one, they took down the wasteful torches that lighted the sky at night and in their place was substituted the fragile, glass-enclosed mantle that bathed the streets in soft, subdued moonlight, the kind of light a high school boy and girl could most keenly appreciate.

With the gas and oil the drillers came, and they were hard on "harmony." At least those who bunked in our old log house were more for disharmony. They were a kind of holdover wild-westerners given to foul talk, drinking, and fighting, a difficult lot to manage; and that very fact guaranteed that the boss would be tougher still.

The boss was Irish and quick of temper, but also a bold and resourceful man, the kind who is master of every situation. At night the men lingered over their cards and their drinks. In the morning it was hard to get them up. The boss called them once, if that didn't work he doused them with fire. More than once I saw him reach his hands into the old straw ticks upon which the men lay, hold the straw to the fire in the little potbellied stove and when it was blazing well toss it on the heads of those who were asleep. It was wake up or burn up!

Somehow it was Christmas which seemed always to restore Harmony to its original destiny. At least, as a boy, I lived looking back to the last Christmas and forward to the next. To an only child isolated in the country, life dragged along in lonely paths. Christmas made up for it with all the aunts and uncles—there was a heap of them, for grandad and grandmother had sixteen children—coming back to the old farm for Christmas Day. Cousins poured in like grasshoppers into a summer wheat field. Pushing and scrapping took place among the younger fry, and sometimes a haughty jealousy was kicked up as we compared our gifts and magnified our virtues. Sooner or later, however, the real spirit of the day predominated and that meant happy hours of coasting, eating, and singing.

When fifty or more members of one family gather in an old farmhouse to celebrate Christmas, it is an event of many happy facets. The enjoyment of a Pennsylvania Dutch Christmas dinner is something utterly beyond words, even though the kids were compelled to wait and starve until the second or third table. Turkeys stuffed with "filling" and roasted "chust so"; the cranberry sauce, the sweets and the sours, fruit salad, mince pies—not the kind with a stick, but just a little splinter—and all those homebaked cakes: Aunt Lena's coconut, Aunt Anna's chocolate, Aunt Tilly's marble cake, Aunt Bessie's angelfood. It was Christmas that brought out the Dutch in Harmony.

Christmas was not a day, it was a season. In the nearby Lutheran and Reformed Churches "Christmas practice" began right after Thanksgiving and continued without letup until Christmas Eve. Every boy and girl had to have a "piece" to say; Grandmother always called it a "Grischtdawgs Schtuck," and the choir—no matter what its limitations—had to exercise and strain every vocal cord singing the good old Christmas carols and attempting the ultra new crackpot music with all its slurs, its holds, and its jingles.

Three or four nights each week we practiced at the Church. I rushed my school homework, Dad got an early start at the evening chores, Mother hurried the supper and we all struck out for the Church, which was down the hill, by the cow pasture, through the woods and up the hill again a good two miles away. Sometimes there was snow and it was fun going in the fast-moving sleigh with a full moon looking down upon us, a buffalo robe pulled up to keep us warm, and sleigh bells to accompany us on our way. More often the roads were frozen and rough and then it was sometimes easier to light a lantern and walk through the woods. This was especially true when the mud was deep, so deep as to peril the horse and wreck the buggy. No matter what the weather, we got there, for Christmas was coming and everyone must be in perfect readiness to welcome it.

However we went to practice, we passed the old house on Scholar's Run, where my father was born and where he celebrated his first Christmases. Often he told me about it, especially the Christmas tree and the family dinner. In those days there was no Santa Claus to venture down the chimneys of the Dutch. Santa with his bulging pack of toys would not have been in keeping with the stringent frugality of the times. Bread and potatoes, nuts and apples, homemade mittens and socks, these were the ultimates in Christmas expectations.

While Christmas Eve brought no dreams of the jolly old elf with his reindeer on the roof, it was sure to provide ample excitement, for that was the night when Belsnickel made his rounds. There would be excitement for all and fear for many; some of the older boys and girls remembered all too well Belsnickel's whip and the sting of the lash.

Belsnickel was not a happy thought. His appearance was forbidding—a black face, bedraggled hair, heavy-booted feet, clothing of rags and animal skins, in one hand a bell to warn of his coming and in the other a whip to provide a stinging reminder.

First he would run around the house ringing his bell, then with his whip he would tap on the window panes; finally he would bolt through the door, making hideous sounds and threatening motions, for his supreme purpose was to scare the daylights out of the kiddies. After prolonged antics he would reach into his pockets and out would come the walnuts, hickory nuts, chestnuts and perhaps a few pieces of hard candy, all of which he would throw on the floor.

The children's hungry eyes were upon that treat, but they could ill afford to forget that whip. Soon the scramble for the nuts and candies was in full swing. Then it was that old Belsnickel wielded his whip "belsing" them on their rears. Amidst the laughing, the crying, and the screaming, Belsnickel made a quick exit.

Though Belsnickel was gone, the fear of him remained. Before going to bed the stockings, all sixteen of them, would be hung at the mantle over the open fireplace in the bold expectation of more nuts and a few more candies, but every boy and girl, my father included, knew that for the bad ones there would be nothing but coal in the stockings. Dad confessed that happened more than once—Belsnickel's doings, to be sure.

A generation later there was less austerity in Christmas, and so far as I am concerned it was always a merry Christmas. It began with the getting of the Christmas tree, one for the church, and one for the home, and many extra branches. Late in November or early December some of the neighbors would go together, hitch a team to a wagon, and drive up toward McConnell's Mills where the tall hemlocks reigned supreme. There they would tramp through the woods to find a perfect tree that would be "chust right" for the Church and others that would answer the needs of the various homes. Taking an ax they would mark each tree with a cross and sometimes they would take their pocket knives and cut initials. Then they would await the coming of zero winds and the deep snows, and when sledding was at its best they would go again, this time with a huge bobsled and frisky horses decked out with bellybands of bells. It was a happy day's outing, a real foretaste of Christmas, and about nightfall the jovial men would return singing the Christmas tree song: "O Tannenbaum, O Tannenbaum, Wie gruen sind deine Blaetter."

Christmas in the Church with a glorious hemlock tree reaching the very ceiling and ablaze with hundreds of lighted candles—it seemed as though there were thousands —was for one boy, at least, the most marvelous sight he ever beheld. I remember looking up at the winter sky and all its twinkling, starry hosts, but God's Christmas lights did not stir me as did the candles on that Christmas tree in Church. There was no babe in a manger, nor was there a eucharist bringing him as close as the sanctified bread and wine, but the Church was filled with the song of praise and with the incense of burning pine branches, for always some of the smaller branches caught fire, striving, no doubt, to mingle their sweet-smelling offering with that of the Wise Men's frankincense and myrrh.

There was the Church Christmas and there was also the Christmas at home. The home tree was decorated with all the old ornaments and refreshed with the new: red candied apples, colored popcorn balls, and yards upon yards of the white, freshly strung popcorn draped from bough to bough. As the shadows of the Christmas evening came on, the family gathered about that tree and together they formed one choir. Someone would take over at the piano and every voice would blend in the Christmas harmony. Father sang tenor, but it was Grandmother's voice that most impressed me. Even after she passed her "three-score years" that voice rang out clear and true as a Christmas bell.

When the candles burned low on the tree and began to sputter out, one by one, the singing ceased and the room that had overflowed with raucous, pell-mell voices became reverently silent. When only three gasping candles remained aflame, Grandmother would arise and say, "In the name of the Father and of the Son and of the Holy Ghost."

We all answered, "Amen." Then Grandmother bent her knees, genuflecting as she always did in the Holy Communion at the Church. Another candle expired and with only one tiny, flickering, uncertain light on the tree Grandmother began singing all alone the traditional "Silent Night":

> *Stille Nacht, heilige Nacht!*
> *Alles Schlaft, einsam wacht*
> *Nur das heilige Elternpaar,*
> *Das im Stalle zu Bethlehem war,*
> *Bei dem himmlischen Kind,*
> *Bei dem himmlischen Kind.*

12—"Ach, Dere's
Plenty Yet"

"ACH, DERE'S plenty yet. Chust go ahead un have anosser piece of pie." These are the words one always hears at a Pennsylvania Dutch table whether in the "inner sanctum," that is, the expansive kitchen of a farm home where you are treated "chust like vone of der family," or in a public eating place, let us say Shartles-ville, where there is no end to either the courses or the "Fressing."

That word, "fressen," though much used among the Dutch, is an embarrassing term that should never have been created. It is a constant menace to the tranquility of the Dutchland. In their vocabulary they distinguish between the eating done by humans and that by animals—people "essen," hogs "fressen." It's certainly a valid seman-tic distinction, but one that every true Dutchman tosses out the window as he pulls his chair up to the table.

If a Dutchman does some fressing, who can blame him? A table laden with "Hinkel Welschkorn Suppe," sugar-cured, hickory-smoked "Schunkafleesch," "Grumbeers Sass," "Sees Welschkorn," "Graut Selawd," "Kupp Kais," "Schmear Kais," "Ebbel Butter," "Ebbel Sass," an elective side dish of pickled "Kuddelfleck"; and all man-ner of "Kuchen": pies, cakes, cookies; and maybe "chust a glass of homemade vine," or a stein of beer to "vash it down so"—such a temptation is more than a Dutchman can withstand. That menu—chicken-corn soup, ham, mashed potatoes, corn-on-the-cob, cole slaw, cup cheese, cottage cheese, apple butter and apple sauce, a snack of pickled tripe for those who like it, and all manner of desserts; is it not enough to break the backbone of the most determined ascetic?

Over the fireplace in our home there hangs a colorful sgraffeta plate that was fashioned by a Pennsylvania Dutch potter, Isaac Stahl, who managed to keep the old potter's wheel turning and the kiln going down in Powder Valley near the source of the Perkiomen long after most of the Pennsylvania Dutch potters had folded. The center of the Stahl plate shows off a traditional Dutch design: a double-headed, double-tailed peacock, or perhaps it's two peacocks in flight. On either side are tulips, and surrounding the entire design these words in fraktur letters: *"Essen ist wor Leib un Leben; Trincken ist auch gut darneben,"* which tells us, "Eating is for the body and for life; a little drinking is also good."

The Pennsylvania Dutchman enjoys the good earth under his feet, the nearby Church or Meeting House where the Saints assemble, the family life on the farm, but perhaps his happiest hours are those spent at the family table, and there are no words that give him greater pleasure than these: "Ach, dere's plenty yet." As he pulls his chair up to the table you will hear him say, "'S maul wassert m'r defor"—it makes my mouth water. At the close of the meal, when the last dessert has been tamped down, he is apt to reach for his pipe, lean back in his chair and remark, "Noch 'm Esse 'n Pfeif Dubak—un dos schtet in der Bibel"—after eating, a pipe of tobacco; and this is in the Bible.

When I first found myself deep in the land of the Dutch, the thing that most impressed me was pie for breakfast. Now that I've long been conditioned by their culture and have come to share the Dutch "stuff" and the Dutch ways, I'm still inclined to think that the most striking thing about them is pie for breakfast. Add to this practice the accompanying words, "Ach, dere's plenty yet," and you have a people none can fail to admire and love.

The only criticism that can be rightly maintained against the Pennsylvania Dutch table is its overwhelming nature. The same is true of their farm markets. The plenty of the Pennsylvania Dutch Country overwhelms you as you walk down the aisles of one of their markets in Lancaster, or Reading, or York.

Some years ago I had the privilege of introducing a cousin to the Dutch Country. Saturday morning at the breakfast table I said, "Now gayn mer an der marrick." I explained to him it meant that we would go to the Lancaster Market and do our Thanksgiving shopping. It was a few days early, but the market would be less crowded and we could easily put the perishables in the refrigerator or the deep freeze. "Here, you take grandmother's basket that has gone to the market for many a year. It will hold more than you can carry. I'll take these two store baskets and lead the way."

When we entered the Market it was for Floyd an unbelievable sight. He was all eyes and questions. "What kind of an outfit is that? Is it Amish or Dunkard?" he asked. I was about to answer when he exclaimed, "Look over there at those kids—little shavers, they're all pants and hats. Wish I had my camera with me."

The Lancaster Market is the place to get acquainted with the plenty of the Saints and with the many different varieties of Dutch, for there are numerous sects and schisms, each with marked peculiarities of dress based for the most part upon religious inhibitions.

The Lutheran and the Reformed are the most numerous. They are the so-called "fancy" people who wear no distinctive garb, and if you are to spot them as Dutchmen, you must do it by their speech, and that isn't easy as these people get around a great deal and some of them have master's or doctor's degrees from the great universities.

Lutherans require little explaining. The Reformed are a kind of Presbyterian, the Evangelicals a kind of Methodist, the Dunkards—have you ever "dunked" doughnuts in a cup of hot coffee or chocolate?—as the name implies, are German Baptists who insist upon baptism by immersion. These are all gay Dutch except for the Dunkards, who are, we might say, half and half. The Brethren, and the River Brethren, progenitors of the Eisenhower family, are also of the half and half kind.

There are also the Schwenkfelders, wealthy and cultured, of Montgomery County; and the Moravians, an equally superior people—if it is possible to speak of one Saint as being superior to another—who excel in music and who live in greatest numbers in the region of Bethlehem and Nazareth. These people, once severely plain in dress, are now gay.

The bulk of the Plain People are the Amish and the Mennonites. The Mennonite clothing is somber and becoming, and not too unlike that of some of the Roman Catholic orders. The more strict and rigid Amish folk, inconsistent though it seems, go in for gay colors. They are especially fond of purple and one will often see an Amish woman burdened with a riot of color—purple and green, or red and brown—with high-laced shoes beneath and a black bonnet to top it all. The cut of the clothing is strictly regulated by Church decree and there is no provision for innovation. In addition to their copious dresses the women wear capes and aprons wherever they go; the men their stovepipe pants with a "barn door" drop behind that can be quickly lowered when necessity dictates.

For Sunday there is little change in the women's clothing except that they wear garments made from the best quality materials. The men, on the other hand, dress up for the occasion in what is known as a "Mootsa," or "Muthze," a split-tail coat of Victorian lines, derived, it would seem, from the days when the men normally went to Church on horseback and found it desirable to button up the tail of their coat so that it would pick up less of the road and less of the horse.

The children's clothes do not differ from the adults except in size. About the time a girl becomes six or seven years of age she is taught that her head must always be covered with a prayer cap. This she will wear as long as she lives, for the Bible requires that a woman must have her head covered while she prays. When working out of doors the prayer cap will not be seen because it will be covered with a bonnet. Being a Saint one must be frequent in prayer; being a woman, the head must be covered.

The difficulty in understanding the intricacies of Pennsylvania Dutch dress was pointed up for me one hot August day as I stood on the Lancaster Square just outside the Market. A loudmouthed woman, with a manner of speech as Dutch as they come, nosed her way to the curb. There were two telltale characteristics: her heavy, awkward words that so often came forth in an inverted order, and her heavier, more awkward physique, with rolls of fat chasing one another as she waddled along. She was the "fressing" kind. It was extremely hot and she was dressed for the weather—tight fitting pants below, a hard pressed halter above, and in between a picture-window exposure. Two Amish women, burdened with sufficient clothing for an arctic expedition, approached. With them were two little boys dressed just like their Pop. It was at once obvious that the younger fry were seldom brought to the city where they could drink in all the sights. Perhaps this was their very first trip. There they stood, eyeing that Pennsylvania Dutch woman—more nude than fancy—their mouths open in amazement, their eyes popping. Oh, if I had only had my camera!

But let's come back to the Market with its lofty vaulted ceiling, its high Gothic windows admitting shafts of golden sunlight as in a cathedral of the Old World. Floyd had been driven to the conclusion that he couldn't master the manner of Pennsylvania Dutch dress in a day. Already the strangeness of their garments, the white prayer caps of the women and the patriarchal beards of the men were less forbidding, for almost always they were accompanied with a broad, friendly smile, and sparkling eyes that radiated good will.

We paused before a stall that displayed turkeys, chickens, ducks, geese, and guineas. At the back of the stall, as on the headboard of a Victorian bed, was stenciled, "Benjamin Stoltzfoos, Intercourse, Pa." Floyd lifted an eyebrow and was about to wisecrack. Benjamin—red beard, blue shirt, white apron—intruded. "Vas vill du haven? Ein turkey, ein goose, maybe? Der turkeys iss nice, ain't?"

I picked out a fat, young hen. Benjamin put it on the scales.

"Vie fiel?" I asked.

"Zat vone cums to ochta Dawler un fuftzich."

I reached for a ten dollar bill but Benjamin, good sales-man that he was, began calling my attention to some of the foods that might well be included in a Thanksgiving dinner. "Vud you like sum dried corn, or Schmier Käse? Or maybe your missus voud like sum Fallowalder eb-bels—dere's nossing besser fer ebbel sass." We answered in the negative, thanking him for his kindness and started down the aisle. He called to us, "I hope it gifs you a happy Sanksgiving. Un here's a "Kupp Kais" fer you to try. It makes gudt, ain't?"

Apples, potatoes, onions, pumpkins on the right; home-baked bread, sticky buns, pies, cakes and cookies on the left, world without end. And there was cheese of every kind, some with an atomic impact; pickled beets, cole-slaw, potato salad, sauerkraut, chow-chow; home-canned fruits, home-canned jellies, home-made apple butter—there it was before our eyes, a panorama of the inex-haustible plenty of the Pennsylvania Dutch. As we left the market, after inspecting about half of it, Floyd said, "Well, I never imagined there was anything like this. We saw just about everything, didn't we?"

I answered in my best Dutch manner, "Ach, dere's plenty yet."

The Farmer's Market in Lancaster is centered in the heart of what is doubtless the most productive non-irrigated land in the world. The Pennsylvania Dutch have tilled these same fields for generations and have so cared for the land through crop rotation and the use of barnyard and green fertilizers that its productivity has constantly increased across the years.

If, however, you have the itch for the wide open places, I must caution you not to anticipate a farm home in these fertile Dutch acres. These farms are passed on from father to son, and if one chances to be put up at public auction, some of the Amish are sure to be there pulling at an ear, scratching a head, or spitting a cud of tobacco juice as a signal to the auctioneer, and the price will go up and up, five hundred dollars an acre, six hundred, nine hundred, until you realize this land is not going to be sold to strangers. The good earth of Lancaster County is for the Saints.

The Amish and Mennonites are land rich. They have no holdings of stocks or bonds and many of them prefer the sock to the bank. All their dealings are cash. The stories go round, and there appears to be substance to them, of Amish, who when they make a sizeable purchase such as a threshing machine or a new farm, deliver the money in tall milk cans. On one occasion an Amish couple opened a can and began counting out the twenty dollar bills, one thousand, two thousand, three, five, ten, twenty—. They had too much money. Whereupon the husband turned to his wife and scolded, "Ach, Mary, du bis al ferhoodled"—you are all mixed up. "It vas dat osser can you should have brought, ain't?"

A country sale is another way of discovering the plenty of the Dutch people. The land, cattle, and equipment run up money totals that are almost astronomical. Then comes the Dutch "stuff" with the antique dealers hot upon the chase like a pack of hound dogs, their tongues hanging out, their mouths watering.

When we arrived at the Hostetter sale they were about to auction a jug. An old slip-ware jug, decorated with tulips and dated 1787, had long reposed in the wagon-shed, where it was a receptacle for stray nuts and screws. It had been emptied of its contents, its face lifted with soap and water and polished with an application of wax. Now it was presented before women of taste and men of discernment, while the autioneer outlined its pedigree of rarity and grace. In no time it brought a cool $100.

Our attention was then called to a dower chest in genuine antique blue, with tulips and "distlefinks" and unicorns. It had been kicked around a good deal and it was full of the scars of time, but the auctioneer rubbed his hand over it deftly and kindly as though he were stroking a purring kitten.

"How much do I hear to start this old dower chest? Examine the hardware, look at the painting and the designs. Here is the chance you've been waiting for, your last chance; you will never again see anything so fine at a public sale. To sell a dower chest like this is a crime. How much do I hear?"

He cleared his throat; helped himself to a glass of water; and then looking directly at the people asked, "Do I hear two thousand dollars?" "Who'll give me a thousand? Do I hear five hundred?" Someone calls out,

"One hundred dollars," and the chase is on.

Then the tole ware, the old painted tin with all its rich Pennsylvania Dutch symbols, is shared amongst the highest bidders. Next it's the Spatter and the Gaudy Dutch china that are auctioned. Then the sale moves into the "odds and ends" of old furniture.

Everyone's eyes are upon the stately grandfather clock that has been uprooted from the hall and temporarily planted on the porch. There it stands, counting the hours, ticking off the minutes, until it will be knocked down in a cold, heartless manner, to be picked up by the hands of the highest bidder, carried off and shoved around, no one knows where. It is obviously a clock of superior breeding: a soft, mellow, graceful Chippendale case of cherry wood and a time piece that continues in its accurate course, to the present moment. The map that adorns its face reveals an antique world with such names as "Ethiopian Sea, Great Sea, Eastern Ocean." The moon it displays high in its bonnet is all but full, for it keeps pace with the moon in the sky.

The auctioneer approaches the clock as a commoner would approach royalty. Having paid his respects, he opens the door in front of the pendulum, exposing some of its inward parts, especially the weights. He clears his voice.

"Ladies and gentlemen, here ye, hear ye! Quiet everyone! Here's the chance of a lifetime to own one of the finest eight-day grandfather clocks in the land. Observe the grace, the proportions. It's all original, even the finish. And does it keep time? Well you're damn right it does, and it won't cost you a cent to set your watch, now. The clock is unconditionally guaranteed. It's all original except the weights. When the Red Coats came over in 1776, the first weights were melted down and shot into the British. That's nothing against the clock. Now let's go."

"Do I hear five thousand, two thousand, one thousand? Come on, folks, let's get the lead out of our pants. Do I hear a thousand; do I hear five hundred dollars?"

He looks over the crowd, draws on a cigarette: "I'm bid five hundred dollars. Who'll make it . . . I'm bid six hundred, seven hundred." Again the chase is on and when the dust has settled the estate is richer by $1100.

Reserved to the last was the Stiegel glass which appeared to be regarded as the finale in a fireworks display. Stiegel glass belongs in Lancaster County, for it is in the nature of the crown jewels of the Pennsylvania Saints.

As my eyes fell upon the various pieces of Stiegel I was wishing that the old "Baron" might himself drive up to the sale as, in those pre-Revolutionary days, he drove over to nearby Manheim in a gorgeous coach-and-six, swept along by six jet-black horses capped with snowy plumes, preceded by eight liveried drivers, and followed by panting, baying hounds. In those days people scoffed at his pretentious manner; it would be different now. Nor could I help but think of this pioneer glassblower, whose wares have never been excelled, how he languished at last in a Philadelphia prison because he was unable to pay his debts. Stiegel glass—there's history, tragedy, and magic in those words.

First to be auctioned is a jigger with polychrome enamel designs. There is the blending of soft colors—a rusty red, a sky blue, friendly greens and yellows outlining hearts, tulips, and doves. Time was when this very jigger filled with strong liquor inflamed men's minds and caused them to throw their money around like drunken sailors. Now the empty jigger does it to the tune of $150.

Finally, there is the Stiegel sugar bowl in expanded diamond design, with a graceful swirled knob, all in deep sapphire blue. There can be little question about its authenticity. The expanded diamond design, the deep rich color, the family tradition connected with this particular piece are adequate to put the most congenital skeptic on the run. Here and there you hear a man or woman confess in quiet confidence, "This is the real thing."

The auctioneer was likewise confident. Slowly and carefully he took it in both hands, lifting it high even as a priest lifts the monstrance in the sanctuary. The sun stooped down to kiss it with its beams and instantly the bowl radiated blue fire as though it were a gigantean diamond of infinite facets. The auctioneer knew his glass and he knew his art. This piece needed no prop of words. Like a sacred mystery words could add nothing to enhance it. There was silence as at a Quaker Meeting. Again I thought of the "Baron" in a Philadelphia prison when one word might have set him free, but his friends were silent. Silence can be more powerful than speech.

Then, in measured, subdued tones, such as are used in the confessional, the auctioneer began to invite bids. They came like a spring freshet. Five hundred dollars, a thousand, twelve hundred, twelve hundred seventy-five dollars for one empty sugar bowl. The auctioneer raised his voice. "Twelve hundred seventy-five dollars—are you all done? Are you all in? One, two" . . . a log chain fell from the fence, reminding me again of Stiegel, penniless and in chains. There was absolute silence. Then the auctioneer, his voice lowered to a whisper said: "One, two, three, and sold to Harry Hoch."

The plenty of Pennsylvania graces the tables of its Saints; it fills to overflowing its farmers' markets; it struts itself at every country sale. There is plenty everywhere in the Dutchland. It is brought out into the open at their annual fairs that come at the close of the summer when the harvest has been gathered in. Whether it's the York Fair, the Reading Fair, or some other in the Dutch Country, you will behold much the same picture. At these fairs one sees all the plenty that is evidenced at their farmers' markets. Add to this the display of cattle, horses, hogs, goats, chickens; the Grange exhibits of produce and handicrafts; the Four-H Clubs; and there is before you such a cascade of plenty that you may be obliged to think both of Noah's Ark containing something of every kind, and even of God Almighty, how after every creative act he was obliged to express his pleasure in the words, "Behold it is good."

There are also plenty of people and plenty of excitement at the fair, and need we add, plenty to eat and drink. The last time I was at the Reading Fair I came upon a picture that lingers in my mind. It took place in the area where all the Pennsylvania Dutch Churches had their tents and the faithful were busy serving lunches and dinners to the ever-hungry people. There was the inviting odor of roast beef in the air, and the smell of fried chicken, but the nearby beer booth and the omnipresent sauerkraut tended to monopolize the atmosphere.

Back of the beer booth and down on their haunches were a Pennsylvania Dutchman and his wife. For them also it was time for rest and refreshment. The woman was of the aggressive type, fat and loud. Four children, one step apart in age, were standing close by helping themselves to the pretzels between Dad's legs, and the popcorn on Mom's lap. The man had a bottle of beer, half empty, propped by his side. In his hand was a bottle of milk, on his arm a baby, with an appetite such as a Dutch baby should have. Mom had the other baby—they were twins. It was his turn to receive the preferred treatment. Mom was fussing with no bottle, but was encountering stiff sales resistance. As I went by she was loudly scolding, "You besser take it quick, or I'll gif it to your brosser, ain't? Cum now, don't be vidervillig. Ach, dere's plenty yet."

There is, however, an even more significant plenty that does not go on parade, that flaunts no price tag, that can be neither bought nor sold. It is the spiritual plenty of the Pennsylvania Dutch and especially of those who are numbered amongst the Plain People and who feel themselves called to be Saints. This spiritual plenty is most evident in the stability and integrity of their family life. There is the love of husbands for their wives, the devotion of parents to their children, the respect of children for their parents. There is little or no divorce amongst them. The baby-sitter is not employed. The aged are cared for rather than put away.

For the Plain People life and love find their ultimate expression in the family circle. They frequent no night clubs and if they stop off at the tavern for a "Schnaps," it's not to tarry there. Life's pleasures are to be reaped at home, so there is much singing in family groups. They play Bible games which demand the memorizing of many verses, and such other indoor games as "Botching," where two people seated on chairs face each other, clapping the palms of their hands together alternately and striking each other's knees as they keep time to the melody of some folk song. They also give themselves to folk art—there is always a quilting for the women, the making of samplers and that sort of thing, and woodwork to challenge the artistry of the men.

There are probably no people who do as much whistling and singing as the Pennsylvania Dutch. Their repertoire includes the so-called "fast" tunes—the secular music of Victorian times—and the older stately German chorales of Bach inspiration, and the modified Plain Song of the Amish. In order to appreciate their musical plenty one should visit the Moravians at Bethlehem during either the Christmas or the Easter holidays.

It was Christmas 1741 when a little group of Saints under the leadership of Count von Zinzendorf huddled together in a crude log cabin and laid the foundations of their New World community at Bethlehem, Pennsylvania, cementing it with the songs of Christmas. Even the cattle that shared with them the crude cabin looked up and lowed as they chanted, "Nicht Jerusalem . . . sondern Bethlehem."

Bethlehem remains the city of song. Christmas Eve and Easter dawn bring forth the Trombone Choir. Their Vigils and their Love Feasts call for many choirs and for the participation of all the Saints in the singing of the great chorales, some of them dating from the Middle Ages and others from the Reformation period. The music of Palestrina, Luther, Bach, Hassler and also Beethoven, Mozart and Haydn are at home in Bethlehem. Music cannot be evaluated by the dollar mark, and to a degree this is also true of much that is Dutch "stuff" such as their pottery, tole ware, and fraktur. There is a spiritual plenty inherent in the opulence of the Saints.

As we speak of this spiritual plenty I recall a Sunday service in the little Reformed Church at Niantic. This was in the days when many of the Niantic Dutch regarded English as a foreign tongue. That day all the conversation was in Dutch. The "Breddich," "Gebaid," and "Lieder"—sermon, prayers, hymns—were in English, but not because the people preferred it that way, but because their youthful pastor insisted.

The "Refameer'd" were not of the so-called Plain People, but in reality this particular congregation was a very plain lot. Their farms were not as productive as those in Lancaster County and I had the feeling that they tried to make up for it by working longer and harder. Some of them were shabbily dressed; all of them had rough calloused hands; most of them were of lean build, with faces deeply etched in lines, as is the way with those who find life hard.

While the people were somber, their Church was gay indeed. It was for them a festival occasion, the greatest of the year, in the Dutch tongue "Habscht Fescht," in English, "Harvest Home." The service began with the congregation standing and singing as with one voice the great hymn that they knew by heart, "Come, ye thankful people, come; Raise the song of harvest-home." Banked about the altar were the fruits of the harvest: vegetables, pumpkins, melons, apples, cabbages, potatoes, tomatoes and onions. There were also bushels of home-canned fruits and jellies, home-baked breads and cakes. It looked for all the world like a farmer's market. There was this difference—nothing was for sale. One part would go to a nearby orphanage, a second to an old folk's home, and the third—a kind of salve for troubled consciences— would go to the Parre in lieu of a more adequate salary. Here is one exception where the Dutch sometimes spread their plenty rather thin. The Parre and his family, God pity them! It would be four weeks of feasting after eleven months of famine and the whole family would share a round of indigestion. And poor Marion, the pastor's wife, she'd be canning in her sleep!

Besides the fruits and vegetables there were the flowers, cultivated and wild; and a perfect sheaf of wheat and one of oats brought to the Lord's House that God might be honored, even as in centuries past the Jews waved the first sheaves of the harvest before the Lord their God. Towering over it all was the tall corn, standing as though it were singing God's praise, and the golden sunflowers suppliant as in prayer.

The best of the harvest display was half hidden by this surrounding cornucopia of plenty—a crate imprisoning a live rooster. It was doubtless his first and his last time in Church, and though his shiny red feather and his sickle-shaped tail provided a Harvest-Home centerpiece that can never be excelled, there was in his manner a certain un-

243

easiness that was communicated in a subtle way to the entire congregation. All eyes, and surely all ears, were upon that rooster. He exhibited remarkable restraint during the prayers and the sermon, but when the choir let the anthem loose Mr. Rooster also let loose with loud, repeated cock-a-doodle-doos.

The service drew to a nervous, uncertain close. Everyone held their breath during the solemn benediction. When the Parre had said the last word, that rooster closed his eyes, expanded his lungs, bent his neck and registered a violent protest. He set the whole Church echoing with a dogmatic postude, "Ach, dere's plenty yet."

/